P9-BEE-240

THE LIFE CYCLE SERIES

Growing Old

years of fulfilment

Robert Kastenbaum

"60 Club"

Nancy Mears – Nov 22/97

Carlene Grunder. Dec 31/97

Multimedia Publications Inc

This book was devised and produced
by Multimedia Publications Inc

General Editor: *Dr. Leonard Kristal*
Prod Mgr/Art Dir/Design: *Bob Vari*
Picture Researcher: *Judy Kristal*
Illustrator: *Diana Sherman*

Compilation copyright ©
Multimedia Publications Inc Willemstad (Curaçao) 1979
Text copyright © Robert Kastenbaum 1979
All rights reserved

First published in Holland 1979 by
Multimedia Publications Inc

No part of this book may be reproduced or quoted or stored
in a retrieval system or transmitted in any form or manner
by way of electrical, mechanical or photocopy recording
without prior written permission from the publishers,
apart from brief quotations in critical articles or reviews.

British Library Cataloguing in Publication Data
Kastenbaum, Robert
    Growing Old: years of fulfilment
    References pg. 122–124
    Includes index
ISBN
    90 6427 001 5   paper
Colour origination: United Artists Ltd, Israel
Typeset by CCC and printed by William Clowes & Sons Limited
Beccles and London

Contents

I   How old is old?

A 13-year-old girl watches as her younger sister and some friends play with their dolls. She has a sudden impulse to join them. Why doesn't she? 'Because I'm too old to play with dolls, I guess.'

Later she races excitedly from the telephone to ask her mother if she can go on a date with a boy who has his own car. 'No, dear,' is the reply. 'You're not old enough for that sort of thing.'

A 60-year-old man is overlooked with hardly a thought when an opportunity for promotion arises. Why? 'He's too old to learn a new job.'

Another candidate, this time aged 20, is also hastily passed over. 'He's not old enough to take on those responsibilities.'

'Old' is a powerful word in today's world. We make many decisions, or have them made for us, based on assumptions about age. We are often made aware that we are either 'too old' or 'not old enough' for activities, opportunities and experiences we desire. In the same way, we tend to judge other people according to their age.

Let us begin, then, by examining some ideas and practices that have become associated with a person's age. In fact, we will have to speak of 'ages' because there are different ways of being old.

The ages of me

In competitive swimming Mark Spitz is already an old man.

First, enter your most intimate laboratory, your own mind. Take a long look at yourself and insert a specific chronological age in each of the following statements. The completed sentences will reflect the way you see yourself at the present moment.

1. In other people's eyes, I *look* as though I am about ____ years of age.
2. In my own eyes, I judge my *body* to be like that of a person of about ____ years of age.
3. My *thoughts and interests* are like those of a person about ____ years of age.
4. My *position in society* is like that of a person about ____ years of age.
5. Deep down inside, I really *feel* like a person about ____ years of age.

And just one more question:

6. I would honestly *prefer* to be about ____ years of age.

No broken records for this man in his nineties.
The race itself is a victory. He shatters the image of old age as a period of physical decline.

Bob is a 43-year-old family man. That's the way he sees himself – at home, anyway. At work, his authority and responsibility as a senior executive make him feel close on 55. But at weekends on the sportsfield he sees himself as still a young man.

How old do you feel?

These questions are part of a research procedure known as 'The Ages of Me'. You might like to compare your own pattern of answers with some of the most typical patterns of response that my colleagues and I have been finding in our research.[1]

Consider first the matter of consistency. The person who gives the same age in all the questions is telling us, in effect, that he has one age and one age only. This is especially clear when the look, body, feel ages, etc. are identical with chronological age.

In practice, however, this seldom happens. Few people, at any chronological age, describe themselves so consistently.

One 45-year-old engineer, for example, judged that his body was like that of a 30-year-old. However, he judged that his position in society was like that of a person about 64 years old. He had no difficulty explaining this discrepancy. With careful eating habits and regular exercise he had maintained his body in unusually good condition. He feared, though, that he was all but through as a 'real' engineer because administrative responsibilities had prevented him from keeping up with the fast-moving field. He was 'old' in the sense of having become dated in his chosen profession, despite the fact that his body was 'young'.

Distinctions of this kind are commonly made by both men and women: older in some ways, younger in others. One of the most typical differences occurs between 'feel' and chronological ages. People in their third decade and beyond usually feel younger than their 'official' age. This remains true of many people in their 70s and 80s.

6

'It's always the other person'

It also became obvious that most people in their third decade and beyond preferred to be younger than their chronological age. In other words, they considered themselves to be too old. There were some people who did seem content enough with their present age. Very rarely, however, do we come upon someone who actually expresses a preference for being older.

It is tempting to shrug and say, 'Well, that is just about what we would expect, isn't it?' But why is this just what we would expect? The fact is that we do have an aversion to old age, but we also *take this aversion for granted*. This deep-seated aversion is found even among people who have chosen to enter the field of gerontology, that is, the medical and scientific study of old age.

In one of our studies, advanced students in gerontology were disturbed by requests to consider their own age-status: they were willing to study ageing and to help old people, but were appalled at the notion of growing older themselves.

'Old', in effect, is obviously something that most of us would prefer not to be. This makes it very difficult to treat growing or being old objectively. A person can say, 'I am a man', or 'I am a woman', 'I have brown eyes' or 'I have blue eyes', with reasonable impunity. But to say, 'I am old', is to court disfavour either with society or with one's own self-esteem.

Would you like to be called old?

I have asked some people in their 70s and 80s what it would mean if they characterised themselves as old. 'It would be like saying I'm not much of a person any more.' 'I'd be thrown away like an old shoe.' 'I have too much self-respect left to say a thing like that.' 'Oh, it would be like asking for sympathy, for pity. And that's not what I want.' Age is so contaminated with value implications that we may hesitate to own up to our years or to refer to a loved one as 'old' for fear of insulting him. Our ability to think rationally about age and make reasonable decisions is coloured by this.

The fact that most people see differences between their various personal ages deserves to be taken seriously. Two people at the same chronological age may behave quite differently and make different life decisions if they have different private versions of their age. In fact the more we know about the full range of a person's ages, the better we can understand him and predict his actions. Chronological age tells us very little about a person.

Old age is not easy to define

What is 'old age' – and how do we define it? There is no simple answer. In fact, there are several definitions and we tend to slip unknowingly from one to another. Here are some of the ways in which old age is defined in theory and practice, along with observations based upon gerontological research.

'How old do you think I am ... ?' The challenge of getting to the truth behind appearances provides this man with his livelihood.

Retired from active duty this soldier serves on, guarding the Tower of London.

Our days are numbered: chronological age

Our days are truly numbered. From the day of our birth onward, our progress through life is tracked by the relentless series of numbers that comprise our chronological age. The usual assumption is that the passage of time, as measured by the calendar, is a reliable index of changes in our minds and bodies and in our abilities and limitations. Yet this assumption is false.

The error is well illustrated by the important example of compulsory retirement. The age of 65 is still the most frequent time singled out for compulsory retirement, although more diversity has been shown lately. A naïve person might believe that there really is something 'different' about a 65-year-old. He might also believe that the age of 65 has become the standard retirement age on the basis of scientific knowledge.

In reality, there is no scientific support for retirement at 65, or at any particular chronological age. Political and economic reasons were responsible for the age-based retirement practice that has dominated occupational careers through much of this century.

Here are some of the reasons why the link between chronological age and mandatory retirement is so unsatisfactory:

1. Within a particular individual, the rate of age-related changes can differ greatly. We shall see, in Chapter 3 for example, that even in such specific realms as 'intelligence' and 'memory' a person is likely to show a complex pattern and rate of change rather than a generalised decline.

2. There are important differences between individuals in the rate and pattern of age-related changes (just as there are differences in how rapidly and evenly we move from infancy to maturity).

3. There is no sharp drop-off in either physical or psychological functioning at or around the age of 65. Strictly on the basis of research and clinical observations, there is no compelling reason for selecting this chronological age as a cut-off point.

4. If we take an individual's functioning apart, piece by piece, we shall often find some deficiencies and impairments with advancing age. Actions that require rapid finger movements, for example, show a decline. But such isolated actions are not vital in most occupations or in most other life situations. Many people learn alternative, often improved, ways of managing tasks and responsibilities with advancing age. Moderate loss in certain physical skills may be more than compensated for by a resourceful strategy for mastering the whole job situation. The worker at the age of 65 may be slower in some physical actions, but actually quicker in other regards because he has a well-cultivated background of experience to guide his perception and decision-making. This is one of the reasons why some companies change production workers into quality-control inspectors, or shift them into other positions where experience and judgement are especially valuable.

Discrimination based on age

When 17-year-olds are denied opportunities and 65-year-olds are ushered out on a strict age-criterion basis we face what Robert Butler, director of the American National Institute on Aging, has long characterised as ageism.[2] This is a form of discrimination that, in its own way, is as dangerous and unfounded as racism and sexism. Chronological age probably exerts a strong hold on our lives for a variety of reasons that include, but are not limited to, ageism as such.

Age is no criterion for the enterprising.

Convenience is probably one of the reasons. Everybody has a chronological age, and it changes in a completely predictable way. It is also one of the easiest personal facts to obtain. People who feel obliged to sort out other people naturally turn to chronological age as a convenient aid. Furthermore, we live in a time-and-number-conscious society. The clock sends us scurrying from one responsibility and activity to another. History is often taught as a succession of important dates; statistics are created and disgorged by science, government, industry and even sport.

But there are other reasons that may cut deeper. Chronological age can be used as an instrument of power and control. The fact that compulsory retirement, for example, has been made as automatic as the machinery on the factory floor relieves the management from having to evaluate a particular worker's status. It also relieves the worker from having to take the discharge as a personal attack upon his motivation or abilities.

Compulsory retirement is sometimes rationalised as a necessity if a place is to be made for the young. However, youth often encounters age-based prejudice as well. Playing off the young against the old may have certain advantages to management, but it is not based upon the actual abilities of the individuals involved. It also ignores the possibility of developing employment plans that would be appropriate for all people.

Emphasising chronological age also stems from other social and individual concerns. Sometimes we fear competition from the older person. One study has shown that it is the competent old person who most arouses the apprehensions of his juniors.

Another frequent concern is priority for the distribution of scarce resources. In many of the developed nations a decision such as this characteristically favours the young over the old. This has not been true of every society throughout history, however, and even today there are important exceptions. Within the ranks of highly industrialised nations, the elderly receive a greater share of the resources and enjoy more respect in some places than in others. For example, in Japan, according to Erdman Palmore:

> The employment status of the elders is much higher than in other industrialized countries: over half the men continue to be employed. Most of those who stop work do so for voluntary and health reasons rather than being forced to stop by compulsory retirement or other discrimination . . . the status of Japanese elders . . . is substantially higher than that of the aged in other institutionalized countries . . . Japan shows that a tradition of respect for the aged can maintain their relatively high status and integration despite industrialization.[3]

In other words, it is by no means necessary to deprive people of their opportunity to work and otherwise be integrated into society because of advancing age. When we do muster people out of the mainstream it is not for reasons well established by medicine and science, but for the sake of our values and priorities.

Another very important reason for wanting to put distance between ourselves and the 'old', to put it bluntly, is that old people remind us of death. Much of the twentieth-century lifestyle serves to help us forget, gloss over or neutralise the ancient proposition: 'All men are mortal.' The person who is not willing or able to face his own relationship to death may have considerable difficulty in being with old people. This is yet another reason for exploiting chronological age, as a way of establishing distance.

Age-grading

Society has an alternative method of classifying people by age. The distinctions are based on a person's life situation, especially the place held in society, rather than on the number of years since birth. Sociologists and anthropologists sometimes refer to this as an age-grading approach. It has been the most important basis of age distinction in many societies, and continues as a supplementary approach in industrialised nations today.[4]

A simple age-grading approach divides the population into the young, the grown-up and the aged. This closely follows the pattern of psychosexual development. People are classified, in

Philosopher Bertrand Russell (left) at a protest in his nineties, and a happy 103-year-old preparing for her first helicopter ride.

effect, as pre-parental, parental or post-parental. Many societies add another category, 'adolescence'. The person is recognised to be grown up in most respects, but still has another step to take before gaining full acceptance as a mature adult.

Different ages, different rules

Age-grading can be as powerful as chronological age in shaping a person's life. The rules of behaviour are often quite different for the various grades. In some societies, children are indulged: they can enjoy themselves with a minimum of discipline. But when they become regarded as adolescents or adults they are expected to be serious and disciplined. The reverse occurs in other societies.

This means that moving from adulthood to old age can have different implications, according to the rules that characterise a particular society's age-grading. Becoming an elder is often an improvement in status for the woman in age-graded societies. She can now enjoy more prestige and power than ever before and can delegate to younger people the chores she most dislikes. In that same society, the prestige of the man is more likely to reach its peak in early or middle adult life, but to shrink when he is classified as old.

Age-grading is important as a way of distributing rights and responsibilities. It establishes guidelines as to who should do what kind of work and who owes what kind of obligation to whom, and so on. In a thoroughly age-graded society, everybody has a pretty good idea of what he or she is supposed to be doing at a particular time of life.

But this system also has its quirks. Age-grading, as a type of social control, can wander away from some of the significant facts of development.

Consider, for example, the relationship between fathers and sons in rural Ireland. The father owns the land and through his possession also retains his authority and status in general. His sons work on the farm and receive not wages but 'allowances' or 'spending money' at the father's discretion. The boys are expected to be as respectful and obedient as they are dependent. This situation would not be unusual if it were not for the fact that the so-called 'boys' could be well into their 30s or even 40s.

Age-grading can work in the other direction as well. If a society finds that it needs more warriors or workers then even pre-adolescents may be judged 'old enough'. Even the aged may be pressed into service. In protracted and desperate warfare, even in our own time, children sometimes have been redefined as combatants.

Social utility

There is a strong element of social utility when a society emphasises age-grading. It has been necessary to legislate against the exploitation of child labour in some 'advanced' societies. People are 'too young', 'too old' or 'just right' for particular responsibilities and privileges, depending upon what society needs at the time.

We have looked at two different approaches to the question, 'How old is old?' The two approaches are not easy to reconcile, although both operate in the societies in which most of us live. Chronological age classification is generally the 'official' technique used to sort us out. Age-grading, however, still tends to play a strong part in our lives. The 'old-timer' may be an experienced worker who is no older chronologically than the newcomer to the job situation. We seem to need people in both junior and senior status in many situations, even if the chronological age difference is trivial, nonexistent, or even reversed.

Functional age

Surely there must be a definition of age that is more 'real', more based on solid fact, than either the chronological or age-graded systems allow? When we say, 'I feel like a _____ year-old,' we are offering one kind of functional definition. We judge that we are functioning like a person of a certain age, whether that be older, younger or the same as our calendar age.

In recent years gerontologists have started to take this approach seriously. Two of the major contributors to the scientific study of ageing have proposed ways of studying functional age. Alex Comfort suggested a battery of no fewer than 55 different measures of physiological and psychological functioning. All of these measures would be taken on the same individual to indicate what type of medical intervention, if any, might be needed.

James Birren[5] has proposed that three types of functional

Craftsmanship and creativity have a lifespan limited only by the ability to create.

Ludmilla Tourischeva ... functionally 'past her prime'?

ageing can be recognised: biological, psychological and social. An individual could be given functional ages in each of these spheres, as well as a composite, overall functional age. The more these three dimensions of an individual's functioning allow him to adapt successfully, the 'less old' he is. One major study is examining functional age in more than a thousand veterans of service in the American armed forces.[6] These are healthy volunteers of various ages who come in for repeated clinical and laboratory tests over the years to be assessed for biological, psychological and social ageing. The findings so far indicate that individuals have a variety of functional ages; this is a clear parallel with what people report about themselves in the 'ages of me' technique that we looked at earlier. Self-report and a battery of laboratory and clinical procedures agree that most of us have more than one 'age' at the same time.

Some clues have been acquired about which components of our total functioning tend to age most rapidly. In the behavioural realm, finger dexterity (as measured by a task such as dismantling a set of objects) shows the most rapid decline of all the abilities studied. Greying of hair is the best indicator of physiological ageing in general, and an estimation of the opportunity for occupational advancement is the best indicator of social age.

Functional age brings a refreshing alternative. The individual

From the busy cobbler to the master pianist, old age can still include an active and productive life.

is justified in maintaining that he is as old as he feels and as old as what he can do. Functional age might well be taken as an optional method for determining a number of decison points in life, such as retirement. A recent study by Frederick Thumin indicates very little difference between younger and older job applicants on a variety of measures. Despite their chronological age differences, they were not functionally distinct. This focuses our attention onto individuals – the talents they possess and how well they have learnt to use them.

Functional age, however, is subject to potential misuse. It would be silly to jump to conclusions about a person because of grey hair alone. Finger dexterity is a useful index to psychological ageing, but we must find a place in our theories for the astounding virtuosity of chronologically old pianists, such as Artur Rubinstein. The functional age approach must be used wisely, and not made captive to an automatic, formula-ridden method of age classification.

Society needs the old

Our society will continue to insist on using chronological age for many purposes. We can live with this practice if we recognise that to set up a chronological checkpoint for calling a person 'old' is simply a matter of administrative or statistical convenience. It is an unfortunate usage, but difficult to avoid. We can minimise the negative impact of this practice by making a clear distinction in our own minds between chronological age and the individual's actual physical, mental and social situation. We can also refuse to be swept along by the implicit relationship between chronological age and human value. 'Ten years older' does not mean 'ten years worse' or 'ten years less valuable'.

Age-grading emphasises society's interest; functional age emphasises the direct facts about the individual. Ideally, both sets of considerations should be taken into account. Problems

arise when a person is not given the opportunity to function as he or she is able because of environmental restrictions, often simply matters of social control. More awareness of these differing frameworks would help us develop flexible pathways through the entire lifespan. Society's need for 'junior' and 'senior' people could be respected, but with less pressing of people into premature responsibility or retirement, or holding them back from opportunities that they are ready to pursue.

It will also help if we bear in mind the difference between ageing and being old. As will be seen in more detail in the next chapter, ageing can be looked on as a process or set of processes. We go on ageing for years and years.

Oldness, however, is a state of mind. It is defined for us by outer standards, as in chronological age, or by our own judgement. We can set 'oldness' relatively late in life. We can choose to regard it as a desirable or dreadful condition. We can just try to forget about it, but I, personally, must leave that path to others.

We shall probably see 'old age' continue to roll backwards for several decades. Until a few years ago, social statisticians and most others were content with 65 as the magic number to mark entry to old age. Now, however, leading statisticians are more likely to move the definition to age 75 : this just makes more sense to them in terms of the length of lifespan and the changing characteristics of the populations in 'developed' societies. Mandatory retirement age in the United States is now in the process of being moved back to age 70, the first significant governmental recognition that '65 and out' is becoming an increasingly inappropriate policy.

In this book we shall use the word 'old' as a general means of referring to men and women in their 70s and beyond. No disrespect is intended when we use the word in this sense, nor does it involve any assumptions about the person's quality of life, usefulness to society, or value as a human being. 'Ageing' will be used when we refer to the process that accompanies us throughout our lives, starting well before old age.

*Advertising tends to
suggest that only the
young are healthy. Such
propaganda can
needlessly
resign us
to decline.*

16

2 Our body and its seasons

Shall I still be able to depend on my eyes and ears? Shall I have the strength to cope with the physical demands of everyday life? Will my heart be capable of its vital responsibilities? My kidneys, liver, lungs? Will my body continue to be able to fend off disease? To mend itself? To respond to emergencies? Shall I be able to count on 'a sound mind in a sound body'? Or will my ability to think straight and to remember be undermined by the ageing process? Can I do anything about what happens to my body as I age, or must I resign myself to an old age inevitably fraught with ill-health?

As we grow older we tend to be more concerned about the functioning of our bodies. We notice each change in our physical appearance. We question our abilities. Physical condition and our preoccupation with it is a vital topic in a discussion of the psychology of later life.

Is poor health really synonymous with old age? What changes in our body and its functions are brought about by age alone? These are among the questions that will be considered in this chapter.

Old does not mean ill

We often associate being old with being ill. There is undoubtedly more physical impairment and illness among 80-year-olds than among men and women half a century younger. Certain conditions are especially common among elders. Arthritis and rheumatism are important examples of the type of physical distress usually described as 'chronic' and encountered more frequently among the elderly. It is easy but not accurate to conclude that old age itself is a kind of generalised illness. Let us see why this conclusion is off the mark, and whether there is an alternative view.

We do not necessarily become vulnerable to all types of physical affliction as we grow older. Asthma, hay-fever and peptic ulcer, for example, are conditions that afflict young and

17

old adults equally. Results of an official national health survey in America actually show a decreased incidence of certain illnesses among adults aged 45 and over. Older people are strikingly less vulnerable than the young and middle-aged to a variety of diseases caused by infection or parasites.

The fact that some diseases respond well to efficient medical treatment sheds doubt on the glib assumption that old age and illness are the same thing.

Another fact to consider is that illness and reduced abilities are not the same even though they are both departures from an ideal state of health. Many of us, at all age levels, lose functional capacity for reasons that cannot be blamed on illness. The person who cannot walk up a flight of stairs without huffing and puffing may be out of shape as a result of a sedentary lifestyle. I know a 93-year-old woman who regularly overtakes a person half her age with a disapproving shake of the head as she climbs energetically to her third-floor apartment.

Loss in various capacities may begin fairly early in adult life, long before a person is supposed to be 'growing old', and without being caused by disease. This means that a low level of functional capacity in an elderly person is not necessarily the result of old age or of disease that is part and parcel of old age.

What, then, are the effects of old age on its own, apart from physical illness and the effects of an unhealthy lifestyle? Is there a biological process that could be known as normal ageing, a process partly hidden by additional deficits brought on by disease, accident and unhealthy life habits? This is the view of many gerontologists. It is difficult to put to the test, especially with humans.

Healthy old age

There have, however, been some carefully designed studies that help to establish the distinction between being old and being ill. One of the most important of these investigations was conducted by an eminent team of doctors and psychologists. James Birren recruited a group of elderly men who were free from illness, as determined both by clinical and laboratory examinations. These men willingly co-operated in extensive studies of their physical, psychological and social functioning.[1] Although all the men (average age 71) were in good health, the researchers were still able to distinguish between the healthiest and the less healthy. In this way, they could see if even minor or preliminary signs of illness had an appreciable influence on functioning.

The results strongly suggest that being old does not necessarily mean being ill. The very healthy old men functioned as well in various physical tests as did a comparable group of healthy young men. Altogether, the old men showed much less impairment when compared with healthy young men than would have ordinarily been expected. Age, as such, did not seem to make much difference in many measures of physical functioning. (This was true for much of their psychological functioning as well.)

There were no differences between old and young in blood levels of white blood cells, haemoglobin, the basic level of blood sugar, and serum cholesterol, nor in type of electrical brain function. The very healthy old men were similar to the young men in blood pressure, in the utilisation of oxygen and the flow of blood in brain tissue.

There were, however, a few clear-cut differences between even the healthiest old men and the young men. Perhaps the most critical difference was found in the peak frequencies of their brain waves. Electro-encephalographic readings indicated that the brain waves of the older men were slower. However, the apparent reduction in tempo of brain waves is not a sign of disease nor was it obviously associated with observable changes in thought and behaviour.

When the investigators looked over their complete set of findings, they were impressed by the negative effect on an older person of even a small 'touch' of disease. An older man who would be considered quite healthy by ordinary standards would show a loss in measures of brain functioning with even a small degree of arteriosclerosis. It was concluded that decreased oxygen consumption and blood flow in the brain were not signs of ageing as such, but had resulted from a specific disease.

In everyday life, however, all too often old *is* ill. Apart from the fact that certain chronic conditions are more common in later life than earlier, there is the additional consideration that many older people suffer from several physical problems at the same time. Multiple illness can greatly complicate both diagnosis and treatment. Also, the over-readiness to take old for ill sometimes prevents the old person himself as well as the family and physician from making efforts to restore health. Studies of this kind emphasise the importance of the prevention and early treatment of diseases in the elderly.

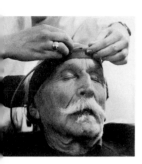

Ninety-nine – and still going strong. Russian doctors, who performed extensive tests on this former building engineer, found his intellect 'practically intact' and his physical condition far better than expected for a man of his age.

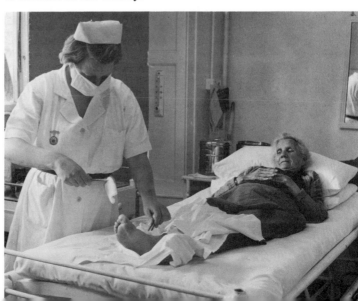

Small complaints, caught in time, can be cleared up before they become a burden.

How the body changes

What are some of the more significant physical changes that tend to come upon us with advancing age? The following findings come from many studies conducted around the world, although chiefly in industrialised societies. All the changes described, however, do not necessarily reflect the working of a pure, universal process of 'ageing'. Illness and lifestyle no doubt play an important role as well. What follows, then, should be understood as the most typical pattern of age-associated changes in the human body. Exactly why these changes come about and what, if anything, can be done to prevent or delay them are separate questions.

Physical peaks – and declines

It could almost be said that when a person stops growing, he begins to age. Some of our bodily functioning may already have passed the peak and started on a very gradual decline while we are still reaching peak functioning in other ways. For example, the adolescent who has not yet completely matured physically may start losing a little visual acuity and ability to respond to changes in illumination.

This means that different aspects of our body begin the downhill run at different times. It is one reason why biological age is not a completely satisfactory concept: we have many different biological ages within us.

There are other individual differences as well. You may not have a grey hair on your head or a wrinkle on your face while your old school chums are clearly showing their age.

The general process of biological ageing can be compared with a long, slow tide that moves upon us so gradually that it may be quite a while before we are aware of its presence. It is a continuous flow, rather than an enormous wave that shatters and engulfs. We learn to swim, and float with or adjust to many of the changes so gradually and naturally that we may not be clearly aware of their taking place. There may come a particular point when we define ourselves as 'old', or when others make this definition, but the process will probably have been going on for a long time. And it is entirely possible to enjoy a long life without ever being faced directly with this redefinition.

There are some exceptions to this. Illness and forced retirement are among the life circumstances that can suddenly focus our attention on physical changes that have actually been going on for quite a while. Our awareness may be sudden and often disconcerting. It is also probable that the rate of ageing itself may be accelerated in some circumstances. Emotional stress and an inhospitable environment can have this effect. One year of exposure to the din of heavy machinery might have the effect of a decade of gradual ageing.

*Many disabilities are
produced not by age but
by our hostile city
environment.*

There are individual exceptions to the principle that all
physical changes after early adulthood are for the worse. President
'Teddy' Roosevelt is part of American folklore not only for his
presidential achievements, but because he transformed himself
from a weak and sickly youngster into an unusually vigorous
adult. He became older, but healthier and more physically
competent. In some cases, individual effort can result in a body
that is sounder in old age than it was in youth.

Yet the typical pattern in the physical sphere remains one of
limitations and decreasing capacity. Here are some of the most
important or characteristic changes.

The ageing body

Older is shorter. This is true for men and women, and for people
of all racial groups. In the single largest study of this theory,
involving 23,000 Canadians, the old men were, on average, 3
inches shorter than the young men, while the old women were
2.2 inches shorter than their youthful counterparts. Some of our
dwindling with age has an anatomical basis. The discs between
our spinal vertebrae shrink, and so do the mucles that support
erect posture. But some of us also develop a slumped bearing
throughout our lives that is exaggerated by age. Detectable loss
in height usually does not occur until the age of 50 or later.

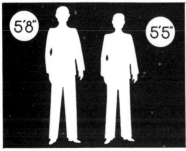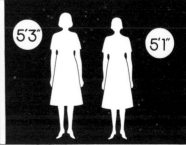

Changes with age can alter beauty without spoiling it.

The gentle exercise of gardening brings pleasure in making things grow.

The outer covering of our bodies displays the ageing process to the world. Although only the thinning, balding, greying hair on our heads may be obvious to the outsider, our body hair suffers much the same fate. Skin changes are particularly conspicuous. If we looked carefully, we would notice wrinkling in healthy men and women who are short of their thirtieth birthdays. In old age we bear the accumulation of changes that have been taking place for a long time, although with increasing rapidity in the later years. Wrinkling and sagging result from a loss of fatty tissue under the top layers of skin, and from exposure to sunlight over the decades. It is also typical for blotches and blemishes to appear. If beauty were, indeed, only skin deep, then there might be cause for lament.

The skin has functions that have nothing to do with beauty, and these are also affected by age. It is brittle and less flexible than in earlier years and does not offer as much protection from disease and infection. An old person may also have difficulty in adjusting to changes in temperature if his skin restricts his ability to perspire and gain cooling relief thereby.

Changes in muscles and bones are far-reaching. The bones themselves tend to lose calcium and become thinner and more brittle. This results in a heightened risk of injury, along with a more limited capacity to make a quick and full recovery. One of the more familiar misfortunes of old age involves the person who falls, breaks a hip, and who from that point on is bed-ridden or crippled. Depression, susceptibility to infection, and a loss of the will to live may follow if sensitive and effective care is not provided.

Our bodily frame is held together and made functional by several types of connective tissue that are more flexible than bone. The type of connective tissue most intensively studied in ageing is known as collagen.[2] It has been well established that collagen loses much of its ability to stretch and 'give' with advancing age. This is the source of much of the old person's difficulty with smooth and rapid movement. Along with the wear and tear that has affected our joints (notably the knees), the impairment in the function of connective tissue can bring about an aches-and-pain feeling of effort that discourages an old person from active use of his body. He is caught in a vicious circle, for the less he uses his body the more difficult and effortful every movement will become.

Although there is a reduction in the number and size of muscle fibres throughout the body, the muscles themselves often remain in basically good condition well into advanced years. Degeneration is not likely unless there is poor nutrition or circulation, or virtually total lack of use. An old person with adequate general health is likely to retain enough muscular strength for most purposes. When there is weakness it does not necessarily mean that the muscles have failed. The problem may have more to do with the overall integration of muscular activity and sensory messages under the command of the central nervous system.

The vital functions

Every bodily function is vital – when something goes wrong with it. Otherwise, we tend to take our bodily functions for granted. We breathe. We eat. We digest. We eliminate wastes. So simple! It is only when a malfunction is discovered that we are painfully reminded how much our well-being and even our survival depends on the good behaviour of our many interrelated organ systems that ordinarily do their jobs unobtrusively. As we grow older, we are less able to take things for granted.

Breathing becomes difficult. As the years advance, it requires increased effort to move air in and out of our lungs. Lung movement is less complete, so that there is more air left in the lungs when an old person breathes out. This means that respiration is less efficient. Among the physical changes thought to cause this reduced efficiency is a decreased absorption-surface within the lungs and a reduction in their capacity for elastic recoil. This loss of efficiency can have serious consequences, contributing to problems in other vital functions.

Cells throughout our body rely upon the oxygen we breathe in and the removal of the carbon dioxide we breathe out. Oxygen starvation or the slow removal of the carbon dioxide threatens the very survival of our cells. The danger is most critical in the brain, which needs a plentiful supply of oxygen. When the supply is reduced through poor respiration or circulation, brain function deteriorates. Thoughts may become confused and disorientated. If the deficit is severe or prolonged enough, there will be structural damage to the brain. The overall result can be a deterioration in the mind and personality, a general lack of co-ordination in physical functioning, and death.

Many old people tend to have intermittent periods of difficulty in breathing. They may have a confused episode because not enough oxygen is getting through to the brain, but recover physiological and mental functioning without permanent damage having been done. Unfortunately, there is a tendency to conclude that an old person is 'senile' whenever a lapse in mental functioning is observed. In fact, many younger adults show similar lapses in mental functioning for various reasons.

Many such cases respond well to various forms of therapy. In recent years one especially interesting form of treatment has been attempted. A person whose respiration has been impaired by age-related or other problems spends some time in a pressure-chamber that enables oxygen to nourish the body without its depending entirely upon lung action. Some researchers have reported impressive physical and mental improvement as a result of these hyperbaric sessions, as they are known. Others have not found the same effects: nonetheless, there remains the possibility that out of this idea a useful therapy will emerge.

The cardiovascular system is another critical link in our

23

survival apparatus. For a long time it has been said that 'a man is as old as his arteries'. This cliché has gained much support from modern research. With advancing age, our arteries tend to become narrower, less flexible, and plugged with various substances that interfere with circulation.[3]

Changes of this kind often lead to a rise in blood pressure. The heart must work harder, even though thickening of the valves and other changes in cardiac tissue itself make it a less efficient organ. Increased blood pressure in narrower, less flexible arteries increases the peril of strokes and cerebral–vascular accidents.

While not all elderly people are afflicted with hypertension, a high blood pressure, this is one of the more common and serious physical problems of later life. It is a condition that sets the stage for death by heart or kidney failure as well as by a stroke. Increased high blood pressure with age is much more in evidence in 'developed' societies. Nutrition, activity level, and perhaps general exposure to stress seem to be important factors. Ageing men and women in New Guinea, Botswana, and the Fiji Islands, for example, do not show the rise in blood pressure after the age of 50 that almost all people in places like London and New York do. But a population with a changing lifestyle (the Papago Indians) is now experiencing an increase in hypertension in later life: the price of entry into 'modern times'.

Diet and debility

Adequate nutrition depends both upon what we eat and drink and how our body utilises these substances. Our entire style of life has an effect. Some of the problems in the digestive process that people encounter in later life reflect more upon bad habits of eating and drinking than upon changes that can be blamed directly upon the ageing process.

Generally, older people take in fewer calories than do young people. This is thought to be related to a decrease in the basal metabolic rate and to a slow-down in physical activity.[4] The tendency is made worse in people near or below the poverty level (a group that in many nations, notably the United States, includes a disporportionately large number of the aged), who fall into eating habits in later life that deprive them of some of the essentials for good nutrition. The elderly person who has an incomplete diet becomes more vulnerable to a variety of diseases, and generally shows a reduction in vigour.

The basic physiological changes in our digestive system do not seem to be as extensive as in some of our other systems. Research in this field has not been extensive, but it has been established that nutrients are still well absorbed and digested. Our small intestines have a remarkable reserve capacity. The liver, with its essential detoxifying function, seems to hold up well with advancing age.

The kidneys fare less well as the years go by. They take longer to concentrate waste products into urine, and are not as effective in helping us to retain a balance of fluids (one of the most critical, if less familiar, vital functions). There is evidence that much of the change is part of an intrinsic ageing process. Even people in good health tend to suffer decreased efficiency in kidney functioning as they grow older.

Bladder capacity also decreases with advancing age, and there may be less awareness of the need to urinate until the bladder is almost full. These changes make the older person more vulnerable to kidney and bladder infections. There is also the challenge to self-esteem when a person discovers, for the first time in his adult life, that he does not have complete control over his bladder. It is possible to help some people regain control, which in turn makes it easier to maintain a normal personal and social life.

The central nervous system

Biochemical and electrical messages crackle through the central nervous system (CNS) almost as rapidly in old age as they do in youth. We have already seen that blood flow and utilisation of oxygen in the brain are unimpaired in healthy old men. These are among the more reassuring facts that have been established in recent years.

However, some degenerative changes have also been observed.[5] The cells of our nervous system have a characteristic that sets them apart from most of our other cells: they grow up and grow old along with us. Most other cells are replaced by a fresh generation – the outermost layer of our skin, for example, is composed of dead cells that have been ousted by vigorous young cells who themselves will eventually be laid to rest on our body surface. There is no replacement for the neuron that dies or becomes inefficient. Most studies, of both humans and animals, find fewer live and efficient brain cells with ageing subjects. There is a corresponding reduction in brain weight and many other changes in cellular composition.

It is likely that the loss in functional neurons is responsible for the slow-down in the electrical activity of the brain observed amongst even very healthy old men. There also appears to be an increased randomness or 'noise' in brain functioning. It is more difficult for the appropriate signal to get through. This could lead to a longer reaction-time to events in the outer world, and more difficulty in co-ordinating the activities of various bodily systems that require 'commands' and 'fine tuning' from the brain.

There are, however, two factors to bear in mind. Because of the fine distinction between simple ageing and the effects of disease, it could be possible that people who remain free of hypertension, arteriosclerosis and other common disorders might also remain free of many of the negative changes observed in the typical aged brain.

The other factor concerns our body's ability to compensate for

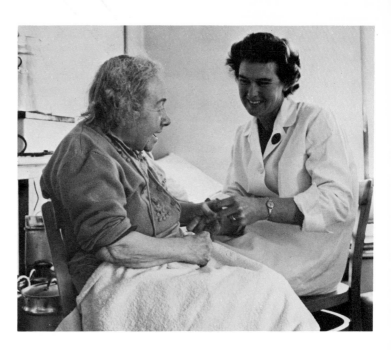

A warm smile, a friendly chat, sympathy and care help recovery from illness at any age.

deficiencies. Compensation occurs in many of our vital functions. When problems with blood flow arise in later life, for example, there is a tendency for an increase in the number of small vessels to serve specific parts of the body. The brain also has its compensatory mechanisms. We seem to possess a considerable reserve capacity and an ability to shift some CNS functions from one pattern of operation to another.

The senses
The senses controlled by the CNS also show many changes with age. *Vision* is usually the first sensory system to show appreciable changes, even in the absence of any particular disease. The lens and cornea become less transparent. Our eyes adapt less quickly to changes in lighting; we are more apt to see spots before our eyes as the vitreous humour (the jelly inside our eyeballs) degenerates. The field of vision shrinks (particularly important when we cross a street or get behind the wheel of a car) and our basic visual sharpness also diminishes. We are also likely to be beset by cataracts and to lose some of the colour that made our eyes look so beguilingly brown or blue.

Hearing sensitivity decreases, especially in the higher frequencies. 'Decidedly unfair,' an elderly physician once complained to me. 'Now that I can afford the highest hi-fi, these old ears cannot fully appreciate it!'

While this is a common finding in most developed societies, there is evidence that in quieter places people show less impairment of hearing with age. The fact that greater hearing loss is often found in men might also be related to their greater exposure to industrial noise.

In practical terms, increased difficulty in hearing human speech, especially when it must be picked out of a context of other sounds, is one of the major auditory problems experienced by many people from middle age onward. The old man who seems to be frowning severely at you across a room brimming with conversation and noise is probably not expressing disapproval of your words – he is simply trying to *hear* them.

Appetite senses diminish with age. Many foods become less attractive in aroma and taste. This can contribute to under-nutrition, and argues for the careful preparation of meals and the establishment of a social atmosphere conducive to enjoyment.

Body senses – perception of motion, vibration, feedback of body positioning and activity – also become less acute with age. Some of this reduction in sensitivity is related directly to ageing but much is probably due to a more sedentary lifestyle.

A good night's sleep often does wonders to restore not only body functioning but a sense of optimism and zest. Unfortunately, research suggests that we do not sleep as deeply and as well as we grow older. There appears to be a particularly important decline in the amount of time we spend in the deepest valley of sleep (the delta-wave phase of the sleep cycle), and in the rapid eye movement phase (associated with dreaming and a pattern of physiological arousal). The old person who half-sleeps through some of the daylight hours may be trying to compensate for the fact that he experienced only half-sleep during the night. Enabling elderly people to enjoy the benefits of a good night's sleep is vital in maintaining overall functioning.

A paradox

We generally reach the peak of our physical prowess early in life – just in time to produce our children and to act vigorously in the world. It is easy to see a relationship between our aims and physical abilities. The long, slow season that begins in mid-life (at about the time when our children are mature and experienced enough to look after themselves) is much more puzzling. Does it mean that we are simply withering away? Here is where we have a choice of perspective. There is more to it than that. The course of our minds and personalities cannot be reduced to biological facts as such. Many people continue to develop as human beings throughout all the years of their lives. It is ridiculous to describe, say, a master statesman, a philosopher or a teacher as withering when he is actually functioning at an advanced level. Despite the season of decline our bodies pass into, we ourselves can continue to flourish and even discover new heights and depths of experience.

This paradox is a central theme of this book. Although we cannot airily dismiss the unpleasant biological facts of old age, they should not be allowed to dominate. Instead of capitulating we must find possibilities for an inner growth and development.

3 The mature mind reviewing and renewing itself

The old man gathers a stack of papers in his arms. Lecture notes mostly – some programmes of scientific conferences with long-ago dates. Correspondence about professional and scientific issues that seemed very important at that time.

He sets the papers down on his desk. Item after item is examined, some swiftly, some with lingering attention. He shakes his head and allows himself a small smile as he finishes with the last paper in the stack. The room has darkened. Almost supper time already! How the time goes.

The old man again takes up all his papers, except for a few he has carefully sorted out, and moves towards the fireplace. There he gently feeds another chapter of his life to the flames. 'Yes, dear . . . I'm coming.'

G. Stanley Hall is the man in the introductory paragraph. He had completed a career of the highest distinction. A founder and president of the American Psychological Association, his teaching, research and writing influenced public thought as well as students of human behaviour. His unusual independence of mind allowed him to extend the first welcoming hand to Sigmund Freud from the stand-offish academic community, and at the same time to criticise what he saw as the errors and limitations of psychoanalysis.

In 1904 Hall offered the first theory of adolescence, which, although it is no longer the dominating view in the field, is still influential. Later he became the first president of Clark University, a prominent educational institution, which still plays an important role in psychology and other scientific disciplines. Hall retired voluntarily.

But his career had by no means come to an abrupt end. His mind and personality continued to flourish. The fact that he was now an old man provided a kind of inner stimulation. The visible product of Hall's final years was a two-volume book entitled *Senescence, The Last Half of Life* (1922).[1] Crafted with mature

Remembering all our yesterdays – planning some tomorrows.

scholarship and veined with challenging observations, this book represented psychology's first major exploration of ageing and old age. It was well ahead of its time and is still unsurpassed for the breadth and depth achieved by one mind in confronting this monumental topic.

A life in perspective
Hall continued to reflect upon life and to enrich his personality. He did not have either to renounce his past or become captive to it. With humour and grace he found himself capable of discarding vestiges of power, physical belongings, and most difficult of all, attitudes and feelings that were no longer appropriate to his situation. He learned how to turn his back on much that had been associated with his long and productive life, without bitterness and regret. At the same time he was able to place into perspective the decades of psychological history in which he had participated. 'How many special themes in my field, once central, have lapsed to secondary importance or become obsolete!'

Reviewing and renewing his mind took Hall into very personal areas of concern: his relationship with his parents, long since dead, and also with those who would survive him. Hall engaged in a scrupulous mental and physical house-cleaning. He also became curious about the physical aspects of old age and decided to learn all that the physicians and biologists of his time had to offer. 'Their books and counsels cost me a tidy sum, but it was well worth it. I now know myself better than they . . .' As his horizon changed, 'he became "more at home" with himself . . .'

This was a person who had long been regarded as having an unusually broad perspective of life, yet he spoke of having changed his horizon again. He was a person who appeared confident and secure, yet he could speak of becoming even more at home with himself. Hall could have coasted for the last years of his life; instead he reduced himself to his essentials and felt much the stronger for it. It was with a renewed sense of strength that he was able to write in his final book: 'I can, at least, speak more honestly than I have ever dared to before, and if I am never read or even venture into print, I shall have the satisfaction of having clarified and unified my own soul.'

Every generation can boast of some elderly men and women who have continued to make significant contributions and to inspire others by their character and courage. The history of music, for example, turns up such names as Heinrich Shütz, a towering figure of the pre-Bach era, and Guiseppe Verdi, both of whom composed masterpieces at an advanced age. In our own times, people such as composer Igor Stravinsky and the conductor Leopold Stokowski retained a strong and productive personality through long lives. There are examples in almost every field of human endeavour. Among those who remain vital, at least two clear patterns emerge: the individual who continues in the direction he established earlier, and the rarer person who creates a new form for himself or his work.

Composing and conducting music, or picking grapes – an active life is a key to contentment.

For example, I have known several women who became widowed in their 60s. Each experienced a strong emotional reaction to the loss. But each went on to transform her lifestyle, taking on new responsibilities and learning how to carry forward enterprises that had always been the husband's province. One completed her undergraduate education and moved on to a graduate degree. All proved themselves ready and able to accomplish significant new learning, despite age and despite grief.

Self-respect at seventy

I also know of a man who had been all but forgotten by society for most of his 70-plus years. Diagnosed as mentally retarded in his early childhood, he had spent more than half a century in a state institution. At the time of his transfer to a geriatric hospital, this man was still without such basic skills as the ability to make a purchase in a shop, or read and write beyond a very primitive level. With guidance and encouragement, he blossomed within a year. He proved himself able to handle small sums of money, make sensible purchases, read the newspaper (with what pride of accomplishment!), write letters and play the oboe. He became a person with heightened self-respect and a glow of accomplishment that he had earned with his own efforts and apparently had never known before.

Mental functioning in later life

According to the 'standard brand' theories of mental development and the most common methods for assessing intellectual functioning, a person will have reached his peak in adolescence or the early 20s. He might be expected to remain at a plateau of intellectual competence for a while and then slide down hill.

However, this picture has proved too simple. The use of more sophisticated research techniques shows that patterns of mental functioning from early to later life are more complex and interesting than was originally thought. Many expert hands are actively engaged in sketching a new picture and some of the more important features are gradually becoming visible.

First, it is important to recognise the multi-dimensional nature of intelligence. Each person is smarter in some ways than in others. He may, for example, be especially gifted in mathematical reasoning, but nearer the average in his comprehension and use of language, and perhaps a little below par in his ability to visualise spatial relationships. This is only one of many possible patterns within an individual. In addition, the relationship between all the dimensions of intellectual functioning may change from childhood through old age. Intelligence then is a living and complex function of a living and complex person, not a fixed single dimension.

As a person ages he may well improve in some aspects of mental functioning instead of undergoing a fairly early and general decline. He will know more about many subjects and become even more skilled in the use of some of the talents he has developed over the years. This shows most clearly in what is known as crystallised intelligence, which is reflected in what we have learned from experience.[2]

Verbal comprehension, for example, is one of the mental abilities that make up the crystallised domain. Verbal comprehension scores do not flatten out and then decline after the 20s: 30- and 40-year-olds showed better verbal comprehension than 20-year-olds, and 50- and 60-year-olds did even better. While this study did not extend beyond 70, it at least showed that some important aspects of intelligence may improve during the second half of the lifespan.

The challenge of immediate tasks

There is another broad set of mental abilities that have become known by some theorists and investigators as fluid intelligence. There are many different aspects of fluid, just as there are of crystallised, intelligence. What they have in common, however, is the challenge of the immediate task. In other words, the individual's stored-up knowledge is not enough to master the situation before him. He must figure things out, solve the

The comprehension of words is one ability that increases with advancing age.

particular problem on its own terms instead of plucking the right answer out of his knowledge repertoire.

Most people show a decline in fluid intelligence over the second half of life, probably a rather sharp decline. Fluid intelligence seems to peak in adolescence and hurtle downward at an alarming rate thereafter. The 30-year-old, still in what many consider the prime of life, has already lost about half of the measurable fluid intelligence that he will have surrendered by the time he reaches 60. A quick comparison of our person at 16 and 60 might reveal a considerable loss of fluid intelligence. But much of this loss occurred well before his sixtieth birthday. In fact, if we wanted to pen people into old age as soon as the ability to master new and unusual problems goes into decline, then we would have to be lying in ambush between the schoolyard and the office or factory. On the other hand, if our focus was on crystallised intelligence – the effective use of knowledge and skills gained over the years – then we could not possibly pin down even the 60-year-old.

The varying patterns of growth and decline for crystallised and fluid intelligence do not tell the whole story. Moreover many of the tests of intellectual functioning that psychologists use may not adequately reflect the changing balance of mental power needed as a person ages. But they do make it clear that our old ideas about ageing and mental functioning may not be adequate.

One way of keeping the young in check! In a game of chess, experience and skill count for more than speed.

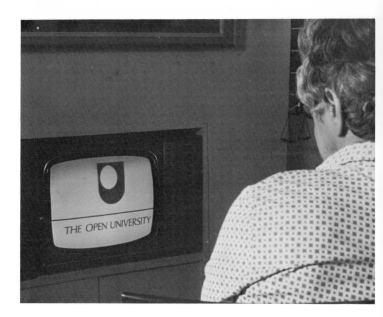

Home study schemes such as Britain's Open University have made further education accessible to all ages.

Learning new things

Virtually everybody remains capable of learning throughout his life. There is no age at which he loses this ability, although due to illness and other factors older people have more difficulty in learning than do younger people. And when it may look as though an old man or woman has failed to grasp something, this is not always because they have not learned but because they choose not to risk making a mistake (a caution which the old share with many younger people). At other times the old person has impairments that interfere with demonstrating what they have learned.

Again, many circumstances can deprive the old person of the opporunity to take in the information needed for both learning and decision-making. The information may go by too quickly, or be made available in an unsatisfactory form, for example, the print too small to read, the voice inaudible.

A person who feels slighted, isolated, or unwanted in a social situation may be too preoccupied with inner distress to pay attention to what is going on around him. This is true of a person at any age, but it is especially true of old men and women in our society.

Whether an old person actually learnt much in a particular situation is not the question. It is whether he is capable of learning. And the answer is yes – given a little help. While there may well be some age-related impairments in learning ability, it is likely that in daily life old people learn more than they are given credit for. They also retain more potential for new learning than they can apply to some of the situations in which they find themselves.

Just how much older people can achieve given the chance to

learn something new, was shown in a study by George Naylor and Elsie Harwood. Harwood and Naylor were struck by the great differences in mental decline and survival among different people as they aged. One study of personnel on the French railway system, for example, found that 20 per-cent of the work force showed virtually no decline, and that these people were the ones who had had jobs which provided a mental challenge.

Harwood and Naylor took a group of 80 old people, with an average age of 70 (the youngest was 63 and the oldest 91), and taught them German. The average IQ score for the group was 118. But although their intelligence level was above average their experience of schooling was well below. Half the group had only primary schooling, and only a quarter had completed secondary school.

After only three months of once-a-week lessons more than half the old people passed a formal exam at a level which schoolchildren normally take three *years* to reach. And after another three months just under half the group passed at the 16-year-old matriculation standard.

Just as striking as their actual achievement was the effect it had on the old people. Naylor and Harwood comment:

> It is no exaggeration to say that the attitude of the majority of our students underwent a revolution before a few weeks had passed. So widespread and deep rooted has the 'old age' stereotype become in our society that it has been widely accepted by the elderly themselves. Those of them who had smiled disbelievingly at assurances of their capacity to succeed ... could not escape the impact of their progress.

'I remember ...'

The shape of memory changes for many people in later life. If our typical old person has one real complaint about his own mental functioning, it is likely to concern his memory for recent events. A word, a name or a fact, just doesn't come to mind when he wants it. What happened in the distant past is likely to be clear and precise in his mind. He can accurately recall events that occurred 60 or 70 years ago, but may draw a blank for what happened a week ago last Monday.

The picture is even more complex than this. Research shows that another type of memory also must be distinguished: recall for immediate events. The old person in good health does not appear to suffer any particular problems in this regard. He can remember what has just happened, can remember very well what happened decades ago, but has difficulty with the time in between long ago and a moment ago.

Why these differences in memory? Current research suggests several processes must function well if we are to have a sound memory.[3] The experience has to register upon us in the first

Comparing and contrasting memories gives an opportunity for new understanding.

place; this is obviously a necessary step both for learning and remembering. Next, the experience must be entered into a sort of storage system where it is coded and becomes part of our personal data bank. But we must also have an effective retrieval system, a way of searching through all that we have on file and coming up with the particular information we need at the moment.

Our childhood memories have had plenty of time to settle into our data banks. However, some of our more recent experiences may fail to take. They fade away before the memory trace can be entered into permanent storage. If we are distracted for psychological reasons or undergo a weakening in the physiological processes that support memory-formation, then incoming information may not make a clear enough impression to become part of the long-term storage system.

Now that we can distingush the different parts of the memory process, we should be able to identify specific problems and come up with specific solutions. Unfortunately, some of the solutions we come up with can create additional problems in everyday life. A person may withdraw from social interaction or a favourite activity because he is afraid that his memory problems will show. Another person may develop habits that make life more complicated (changing the subject or picking an argument when he fears that his memory will be tested). Others borrow, bend or simply invent facts to replace those that do not come easily to mind. More satisfactory adjustments are usually made by those who acknowledge their memory problems and neither surrender to them nor try to cover them up.

Doing things at a slower pace

The ability to contemplate is something that comes with experience, and brings wisdom with age.

At last, time to enjoy the grandchildren.

There is another common change in us as we grow older: we slow down. This change is probably most obvious in physical activity. But it is part of our mental life as well. Psychomotor speed, as psychologists often call it, is required by many activities. This is the pace at which we carry out all steps of an action, from sizing up the situation, figuring out what we want to do about it, and finally doing it.

Activities and tests that place a premium upon speed often show the old person at a marked disadvantage. He does not perform as well as younger people. But does performance in those circumstances reflect intelligence? When activities or mental tests are designed so that speed is not a significant factor, then the difference between old and young becomes much slighter. The old person reveals his ability to learn, think, remember and solve problems when not being rushed and when allowed to proceed at his own pace.

It makes sense to respect the general difference in psychomotor speed between young and old adults. Although there are occasions when raw speed is critical, like dodging out of the way of a careless driver, judgement, experience and a sense of purpose often count for more than a rapid dash to nowhere in particular.

It can also suggest ways of functioning and enjoying life with less dependence on speed and more upon personality and

intelligence. A decline in psychomotor speed would not be so noticeable or important in a society that is free from the hurry-up dynamics of our own. Other cultures have not bothered to divide the day, the hour, even the minute and the second, as relentlessly as we do. Nor do they set rigid starting and finishing times for so many activities. Slowing down has been rediscovered by many people as a more relaxing, perhaps more human, mode of life. Our inclination to slow down in our later years may be nature's way of allowing us to appreciate the scenery of life's journey instead of hurtling toward our destination.

Keeping a keen mind

Why are some old people more keen-minded than others? In youth and middle age some people are more mentally alert and vigorous than others. Keen-mindedness tends to be habit-forming, a combination of fortunate genetic endowment and a lifestyle that keeps the intellect well honed. Evidence suggests that those who start off with strong mental assets are more likely to preserve them throughout the total life span. It is not just that their functioning remains relatively high because it started high, but it is also because the rate and amount of falling off appears to

His body may be frail – yet his mind is still keen, avidly absorbing stimuli around him.

be smaller. In fact, studies of very bright people throughout their lives indicate that growth may continue indefinitely in some areas and show little if any decline in others.[4] How we make use of what we have also seems to be important in the mental as well as in the physical sphere. The athlete who 'goes to pot' can be compared with the intelligent person who does not discipline and develop his thought or gird himself to meet mental challenges.

Attitude and expectation play important roles here. Our society usually calls upon children to live up to expectations, but upon old people to live down to expectations. If we do not expect a person to keep up with current events, to make responsible decisions, to continue learning, to create and innovate, then why should he expect this of himself? The 80-year-old may have nourished for many decades the expectation that 80-year-olds do not think very well or enjoy life very much. He becomes the victim of his own expectations. It is the rare individual who can transcend the climate of such attitudes.

But there is no reason to suppose this effect starts in old age. How many people continue to expect creative thoughts from themselves and others in middle age? Does our family life, our work, our culture in general reward us for reflective thinking, for innovation? Looking back even further, do we leave school more interested in learning than when we entered? *It is possible that the mentally inert old person is victim of experiences throughout his life rather than the product of any new problems encountered during his old age.*

A striking example of the effect of cultural expectations about intellectual functioning in old age is provided by anthropologist Renaldo Maduro.[5] He found that the oldest members of a painters' colony in northern India were also the most creative. Artists in the Brahmin tradition were encouraged and expected to develop both themselves and their art through their entire lives. By contrast, the classic studies of creativity in the West show that we reach our peak quite early and then more or less hang around. Cultural expectations do not ensure that all people will continue to develop their mental resources throughout life, nor do they prevent some people from doing so even when expectations are negative. It is clear, however, that the quality and zest we bring to our mental life in old age has much to do with the climate of expectations.

4 Awareness of the passing years

It is Sunday afternoon. An old woman, dressed in her finest, walks three long blocks to the bus stop. She doesn't mind the overcast skies and the light rain falling. This is a special day. The bus finally comes into sight and pauses near the curb with its usual impatient rumble. The woman dislikes hurrying, for it takes the style and dignity out of a treasured occasion but she fears a punishing look from the bus driver if she keeps him waiting.

With one foot up on the boarding platform, she suddenly pauses in confusion. What is she doing? Can she have forgotten that Gloria doesn't live there any more? Can she have forgotten that she now has nowhere to go on a Sunday afternoon? The bus driver grumbles and glares at her as she slowly dismounts, regains her composure and moves with empty eyes toward her empty apartment.

Consciousness of ageing is more often stimulated by specific encounters with the outside world. These usually come in the form of major changes in life situations which the person has never experienced before, such as admission to a home for the sick or debilitated aged. The encounters can also be as small and as private as catching a glimpse of one's reflection in a mirror. In ways that are obvious or subtle, public or private, the individual is suddenly reminded that life is not quite what it used to be. Each of these reminders offers an obligation for a possible redefinition of the self.

The old woman who hesitated as she boarded the bus was engaging in public behaviour (the stopping, the look of confusion, the retreat), but the experience was a private one. From the outside we could not know what situation she was confronting, nor the decision she made. It often happens that a person's most critical encounters with ageing-awareness are in the privacy of his or her own thoughts and feelings. We may notice changes in attitudes and behaviour, but will probably not understand the experience that has generated them.

The simple fact that time marches on and the years pass by does not necessarily make a person aware of ageing.

Drawing strength from the past

The past is an obvious resource for a person who has accumulated a long life of varied experience. Some of us are more successful than others, however, in the ability to use our own history to enrich our old age. Consider several of the most common techniques that are employed to draw strength from the past and how each of these can yield either favourable or unfavourable results.[1]

Awareness of ageing sometimes shakes the person's self-confidence. Years ago, as an adolescent, he may have known a fierce need to prove himself – to himself, as well as to others. Now the need has risen again, although the circumstances are different. In an effort to bolster his confidence the old person will often search his past. He will try and reassure himself with the thought: 'I have been doing that all my life: of course I can do it again! People have respected me; why shouldn't they still respect me?' Moments of triumph are brought to mind; records of accomplishment are reviewed. *If* the validation process is successful, then the individual has renewed faith in his own competency. This confidence helps him to carry on and continue to demonstrate his competency.

But the validation process is not always successful. Moments of failure may come to mind; regrets and limitations may stand out more strongly than positive achievements. The individual may remain lost and disconsolate amidst the wreckage. The motivation and confidence necessary to move forward with life may dissolve.

'Those were the days ...'

Setting new boundaries . . .
'Forget it Fred,
what was, was.'

Similarly, bias against the elderly may cause others to reject the individual's claim of competence even when he has confirmed it for himself. A few humiliating and destructive experiences are enough to convince some people that they are no longer valid as first-class citizens and it is not even worth while to bolster themselves with credits from their successful past.

Setting new boundaries

This is what happened to the woman boarding the bus. Gloria didn't live there any more. This meant that a navigational pathway had lost its relevance. Gloria's house and all the physical space between her friend's former residence and her own no longer existed for her. 'Sunday afternoon' also lost its special status.

The real boundary-setting had to take place within the old woman's mind. Painfully she had to detach herself from what had long been a high point in the week. And this tightening of her personal boundaries raised new questions about what still remained in her life. She felt more impoverished as a person. Yet once she had regained her composure she also felt a little stronger. Somebody else might have boarded the bus.

Because boundary-setting is such a personal and often such a private process, it can take many forms. Each individual must determine whether a certain aspect of his accustomed life must now be detached and consigned to the past. For example, a physical impairment may lead a particular person to conclude that many activities and relationships must now be dropped. She can no longer go bowling or prepare meals; he cannot take long walks or work on his favourite hobby. Each experiences a restriction to both physical and social life.

43

The reaction to admission to a sheltered housing project or to a nursing home may show what happens when some people are unable to reset their boundaries. The keen sense of having lost an entire world may cause such distress that the individual may respond by keeping his previous world alive in memory at the cost of ignoring the reality of the new environment and its inhabitants. Another individual may respond to the same objective situation by firmly shutting out (as best he can) almost all memories of his former way of life. He will focus only on the immediate scene around him: it hurts too much to think of what has been lost.

Boundary-setting is an adaptive process when the person makes realistic assessments of what can and what cannot remain part of his active life. At least some of the loss may be replaced by new interests or heightened attention to the possibilities that remain. Instead of taking long trips, for example, he may discover the pleasure of painting scenes closer to home.

The process can, however, have unfortunate results. A person may too readily surrender regions of his life that he still has the capacity to enjoy or to recapture. Resistance to setting boundaries and letting go of some past elements of life can also create difficulties. For example, a person may expose himself to serious physical hazard by not acknowledging new limitations.

Keeping the past alive

Moments in history brought back to life; a re-enactment of a battle from the American Civil War.

Anthropologists have described ceremonies in many parts of the world during which a group of people keep their collective past alive, for example by a drama-and-dance enactment of the origin of the world or a great battle victory.

We do not have to look to far-off lands for examples of the ritual perpetuation of the past. The chances are that we do it ourselves – and will do it even more as we continue to age. At times this keeping the past alive exercise is carried out by groups such as alumni or veterans, but more often it is a task each person does for himself. There is an enormous diversity in past-perpetuating behaviour. Recalling a loved one may involve as little as a once a year observance of his death, or as much as keeping a room set aside and waiting for his return. We may perpetuate the past by the way we speak and the clothes we wear. Our actions may be so obvious as to invite curiosity and perhaps ridicule, or so subtle that only we ourselves know what these little actions mean.

A moment of reflection: a loved one recalled.

There may be powerful reasons for this behaving as though past is still present. The last surviving member of a family, for example, has the responsibility of keeping an entire family history from perishing. Nobody else will represent all those lives and keep them preserved in memory. There are few readily available avenues for sharing personal and family recollections with our present- and future-conscious society. Perhaps it would be to the advantage of society to have some specialists around to represent the past. We scrap and discard many material items; 'planned obsolescence' is a familiar commercial strategy. We treat the past as disposable. Yet if we valued it more, then the individual man or woman who cherishes and represents certain features of the past would become more a part of the mainstream of social life.

Perpetuation of the past is unhelpful when the 'pastness' itself is denied. The existence of this process in a particular person does not necessarily indicate weakness or pathology. We must understand the role of past-perpetuation in the individual's total life situation.

The point of 'replaying'

Some elderly people contribute to their own isolation by boring people with tales that are more than twice-told. This is one of the most common characteristics complained of by people who say they do not like to be with the aged (although old people by no means have the patent on repetitious speech).

But there is more purpose to this replaying of the past than might fall upon the bored ear. Notice that the scenes retold are very selective. Often these prove to have an integrating function for the individual. They serve to give the person something to organise himself around. Furthermore, replaying can be the effect as well as the cause of social isolation; in a deprived, alien, unwelcoming environment, the old person may have little other choice but to call upon his own memory repertoire if he is to have any company at all. This is akin to the effect that sensory deprivation has on a person of any age: the mind takes over and furnishes the stimulation which is absent in the environment. But once replaying has been strongly established, it may then serve to increase the individual's isolation.

At least two other features of replaying deserve attention. The memories typically are taken out of their original time frameworks. It is not especially important when they happened. In fact, the whole structure of time that seems so important to our society is de-emphasised. The old person who replays selected memories has often stepped (at least temporarily) out of the conventional time framework. Time has already served its purpose. It has brought forth many experiences from which the

England's village green cricket is a living national tradition.

individual chooses a few that have particular significance. The distinction between 'recently' and 'long ago' is of little consequence. Neither is there much distinction between past and present, or past and future.

The second feature of replaying is evident when the past begins to submerge both present and future. This is an effective attempt to evade the prospect of death – for it is the future that holds death. If one can replace present and future with selections from the past, then no place is left in the awareness for death and the concerns and anxieties associated with it.

Occasional replaying may be a comfort and consolation to the old person. It is most likely to occur when his environment offers little human nourishment and when mental functioning has been somewhat impaired (these two factors themselves often seem to be related). A moderate devotion to replaying can alert us to the old person's need for more stimulation and sharing. The person who seems to dwell persistently in the past may be suffering from marked organic impairment, or having difficulty in facing his future, or both.

Past, present and future all submerged in the vastness. Chronological age means little in a world without clocks.

47

Sharing the past

There can be much satisfaction in sharing with an old person his reflections on the past. Directly or indirectly, it is part of our history as well. Apart from the facts we could glean, it deepens our understanding of life's experiences. Together with the old person, we feel the transformation from child to youth to adult and beyond. In this way each old person who opens his mind and feelings to us is a unique text on human development and ageing.

When we show interest in an old person's past we can be helpful to him in several ways. The opportunity to air out his experiences makes it easier for him to develop a fresh perspective on them. The process of discussing his past with another person enables him to be more objective: he can stand back and take another look at the experiences that have been so close to him. Some of the disappointment and resentment that may have been influencing his view of his past life may be alleviated through the sharing process. This can encourage not only a more positive assessment of the past, but also a more hopeful attitude toward present and future. He may also find it easier to think positively about his achievements if somebody else is at hand to confirm them.

There is no age restriction on turning to the past for help to meet challenges of the present and future. Some of the apparent overuse of the past, shown by certain old people, is related to their reduced opportunity for sharing experiences with others, as well as to reduced stimulation and opportunity in the present environment.

Despite this concern with the past, the future is of interest to many old people just as the past is to many of their juniors. Research with adults indicates that the most typical daydreams centre around practical tasks and challenges and this is as true of old as of young and middle-aged people.[2] The old do not bury themselves in the past or avert their eyes from the future.

Age barriers break down when the past is shared.

Life in review

G. Stanley Hall, the old professor described in the preceding chapter, was examining his total life experiences with his prospective death in mind. He did not expect to die right away. Nevertheless, he judged that it was high time to set his house in order. This is known as the life review.

The outcome of an old person's life review is by no means guaranteed. Like all the other ways of using the past, it can have either favourable or unfavourable results. If the individual is hard on himself, he views his life as a string of failures, missed opportunities. He dwells on his shortcomings as a child, a spouse or a parent and perhaps brands himself guilty of a moral transgression that has not been rectified or forgiven. Such a negative verdict on the kind of life he has lived is apt to heighten his concern about death. He may feel that he cannot go to his grave until he has somehow redone or undone the most unacceptable actions of his past.

At the same time he may feel powerless to make amends, and face the prospect of death (and perhaps the afterlife as well) with dread. The same harsh judgement of his life may lead him to seek death instead: since he is such a worthless person, why continue to live?

By contrast, a favourable life review prepares the way for a more serene attitude toward death. When a person is able to accept the overall pattern of his life with equanimity, he can relax and enjoy the days that are left. Death can be looked upon as a natural, non-threatening end to a worthwhile existence.

What is it like to be old?

Much of the answer can be found in the kind of person we are *now*. Ageing does not take hold of us like some powerful outside force that bends our personality this way or that. More often we continue to work upon our own experiences and cope with our own life challenges according to the patterns set in earlier years. True, most of us will undergo some of the same objective changes such as greying, wrinkling, altered occupational and financial status, and so on. But what these changes *mean* to us will depend much upon the way we have learned to interpret life in general.

This does not mean that our personalities remain constant with age. But the directions and extent of our changes with age should be seen in relationship to the type of person we have been all along. Some people remain relatively fixed in their ways from mid-life onward. Others show a pattern of openness to experience that continues through old age. They become a broader and deeper version of the sort of person they were at an earlier time.[3]

Although the quality of experience in old age depends much

Face to face with old age.

upon the individual, it is interesting to examine the patterns revealed when a large number of elderly men and women are asked to describe their experiences. A major survey of this type was conducted for the American National Council on Ageing by a leading private research organisation. Using a careful sampling technique, more than 4,000 interviews were conducted with people ranging in age from 18 to over 80.[4]

'Things are better than I thought they would be'

The assumption that old age is a time of unmitigated misery took quite a beating from the results. Older men and women reported almost as much *life satisfaction* as did their juniors. In fact chronological age by itself was a poor indicator of satisfaction. Knowing a person's age did not provide a reliable clue to his or her quality of experience at the present time. Income, education and employment status were far more powerful indicators of life satisfaction. An old person with a reasonable income, high level of education and opportunity to continue his employment generally expressed more life satisfaction than the younger person of more limited income and education, especially if he was unemployed at the time. In other words, when a person has had the advantage of favourable background experiences (education being one example) and still has the opportunity to continue his lifelong style (income and employment as examples here), then merely being on in years seems no obstacle to life satisfaction.

By far the greater number of elderly people in this survey agreed with the statement that 'the things I do are as interesting to me as they ever were'. They also felt fairly well satisfied with the life they had been living, and felt that they made a good impression on others. This is certainly not consistent with the view that most old people suffer from poor morale. Most old people did *not* judge that they were now in the best years of their lives, but neither did they describe this as 'the dreariest' time, or a boring and monotonous period.

There was, in fact, general agreement with the following two statements: 'I've got pretty much what I expected out of life,' and, 'As I grow older, things seem better than I thought they would be.'

The elderly generally saw themselves as friendly and warm, wise from their experiences and alert and adaptable. Those with strong educational backgrounds were even more likely to describe themselves in these favourable terms and to report high life satisfaction. Possibly the knowledge and outlook gained from early educational experiences may yield some of their most important benefits in old age.

The overall pattern of findings is encouraging. People who are actually chronologically old continue to discover satisfaction in life. Like anybody else, they are more apt to feel satisfied if they can maintain the activities around which their lives have been organised and do not have to worry excessively about finances.

They are happier when they enter old age with a mind well stocked with knowledge, ideas and successful prior experiences. Generally, older people report themselves as enjoying life rather more than they had thought they would, and more than younger people imagine to be the case.

We should not take all these favourable findings at face value, however, for some old people are reluctant to admit negative feelings. They put on a bright front, possibly to avoid being pitied. Perhaps they are reluctant to admit failure or to burden others with their difficulties in case this should lead to further isolation and rejection. Nevertheless, it is obviously false to assume young people have all the delights and old people all the miseries. Satisfaction is possible at all ages. The difference between contentment and despondency seems to depend more on the challenges and opportunities present in the immediate life situation.

New snapshots from old hands. New memories to add to well-stocked albums.

5   A place apart?

It's an ordinary day. Yet even in its ordinariness there is pleasure. The morning shower: not too hot, not too cold. Breakfast so easy to prepare. The newspaper at the door. The attractive lobby and nearby park with its friendly and familiar faces. Shops within walking distance. Reliable transport easily available for more distant trips. In a place of their own where privacy is respected but where the door can be opened for companionship they have the secure knowledge that they are part of a network of mutual protection, of people looking after each other. They have the help of modern technology to make their lives easier or to summon speedy response to emergencies. Their lifestyle is their own. Best of all, each day opens to them as a generous gift from time, to be enjoyed in a space that feels like home.

The everyday can be a cause for celebration: an ordinary drink when thirsty, an ordinary shelter when the rain is beating down. Many of the difficulties encountered by old people are caused or intensified by lack of the basic amenities that give daily life a secure structure. A social and physical environment that meets the old person at least halfway does much to sustain self-respect, morale and competence.

Settings for lifestyles

Think about the ordinary scene described in the opening paragraph. These two contented people are secure in the knowledge that they are safe from physical hazards. They have a non-skid floor in their shower and bath. Water temperature is automatically controlled to prevent accidental scalding. The controls on the kitchen oven are in front of the burners, so there is never any need to reach over a hot burner. There are safety shut-offs for gas burners. Throughout the building, raised thresholds have been eliminated. There are no barriers to trip over. The doors themselves do not swing closed with enough force to topple over a feeble or unsteady person. A special courtesy is shown by the elevator doors: they close slowly and gently, and reopen rapidly when necessary. Handrails and grab-bars are found at every place that one might feel the need for a little security, leverage or steadying.

Hand in hand, this old pair show that a couple that stay together make their own place apart.

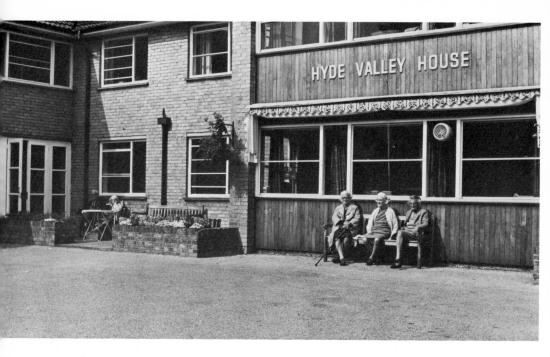

Companionship in the sunny courtyard of a modern and well-equipped day centre.

The entire living environment has been planned in such a way that accidents, dangers and inconveniences have been reduced to a surprisingly low minimum. This extends from a sophisticated security system to discourage intruders to the lag-time switch that grants time for walking across the room at night before the light goes out.

Taken one at a time, the design features are mostly small and common-sensical, although advanced technology is called upon where appropriate. But taken together, the careful design of this apartment house helps the elderly residents to keep their lives in their own hands. They can live independently longer, more fully, and with less effort because the environment is so hospitable. Yet there is ample flexibility : the residents can pursue their individual lifestyles rather than conform to a fixed master plan. For the special features designed into this environment are generally so unobtrusive that their effects are best measured in terms of what does *not* happen – the accidents and misadventures that otherwise might disrupt patterns of the independent living.

Many of the designs to improve living conditions for elderly people can also be valuable for others. As society inventively plans hospitable environments for the elderly it produces ideas and techniques that have a broader application. Nevertheless the particular arrangement described here would not appeal to all old people. No single type of residential setting will suit the lifestyle of all the aged. How could it? Old people should have a range of options from which to make personal choices.[1]

Yet there is often little choice for them today. They are often forced to cling anxiously to housing that is far from ideal. Taxes, inflation, illness, and the type of 'progress' that involves tearing down residences and changing the character of neighbourhoods, are among the threats to an old person's maintaining his lifestyle in today's world.

As important as the physical setting of daily life is to all of us, regardless of age, this is only one aspect of our place in society. It is certainly one of the more visible aspects. There are marked differences between the elderly men and women who continue to live comfortably in good quarters they have enjoyed for years, and those who reside in new housing especially designed for their convenience and those who are trapped in hazardously sub-standard dwellings in deteriorated environments, or who are set apart from the rest of the community behind the doors of an institution. However, we must go deeper than this to have a full understanding of the old person's place in society and how it influences and is influenced by his or her individual needs and resources. Perhaps the most critical influences to consider are those that effectively exclude old people from the mainstream of social life.

Lonely isolation, surrounded by the worn trappings of a worn-out life – contrasting with congenial clubroom activities in a welcoming environment.

Step aside: Forces of exclusion

The role of grandad often gives an old man a new sense of purpose and usefulness.

A person can be more or less integrated into his society. Do people expect many things of you – to be certain places at certain times, to carry out certain responsibilities, to accomplish certain things? The more often you nod your head to questions such as these, the more likely it is that you are highly integrated into society. What you do and how you do it makes a difference in the world. The awareness of being well integrated into society can bestow a feeling of deep security. The integrated person knows that he is 'somebody' because he is treated as such. He can see that he is useful. He takes part in at least some of the decision-making and has access to many privileges and opportunities.

Social integration, however, can be experienced as burdensome and oppressive. A person may feel there are too many obligations to meet, too much time pressure, too many expectations. This, of course, can make one determined to have a break, to take a holiday and Get Away From It All. As we age we have a tendency to opt out – to let It All get away from us. We may find ourselves less socially integrated. We have vacated our place in life, although we would not describe ourselves as on vacation. Some social scientists regard this as a process of *disengagement*.

During the middle years of our lives we are at the peak of our engagement with society. Many people depend on us; our time and energies are in great demand. We are, in essence; the Establishment. This is one of the ideas incorporated in disengagement theory, formulated and introduced mainly by Elaine Cumming and William Henry.[2] They examined the results of a study of normal, community-dwelling elders in a large, rather conservative American city (Kansas City). It seemed to Cumming and Henry that the transition from adulthood to old age involves a natural withdrawal from activities and obligations that previously had linked individual and society so closely together.

Think of a ritualistic dance. One partner (the ageing adult) bows and takes a step back. The other partner (society) takes the cue, returns the bow, and also takes a backward step. The dance continues, but at a slower pace, and with the partners gradually moving further apart. Soon society is whirling around with a new partner, while the old person settles into a chair next to the wall. There he occasionally smiles and nods to the active dancers and taps time with his fingers, but his thoughts and feelings are turned ever inward. He has become – by both his choice and society's – a rather more private person who is willing to leave the high-stepping to others.

A new stability

This is a picture of normal disengagement, or so goes the theory. Both the individual and society are ready to loosen their ties at the same time. After enough mutual withdrawal has occurred, the older individual and his society develop a new equilibrium: still important to each other, but not in the critical, everyday sort of way that was true earlier in their relationship. When the disengagement process goes smoothly, both partners get what they need. The old person has time to pursue interests and activities that had to be set aside during the peak years of social integration. He can dress, speak and act just as he prefers, rather than having to please a boss or fit into general expections. The old person continues to age. Ill-health and other life changes usually lead to further extremes of disengagement, with death the final move. Society meanwhile has had time to teach its new partners their intricate steps of mutual obligation and to prepare itself for the eventual final departure of its former partners.

The theory tries to explain why men and women move somewhat differently along the disengagement pathway. The man is more likely to face the break from his previous life pattern

'Remember when I was the belle of the beach . . . ?'
'You still are, my love.'

when he ends his employment, or when it is ended for him. A typical man is regarded as a person who has organised much of his sense of value upon his ability to provide financially for his family and to live up to his job responsibilities.

The woman, by contrast, is seen by disengagement theory as more of a specialist in social relationships and states of feeling. She keeps the social – emotional or expressive side of life going while her man undertakes instrumental activities. In one sense, disengagement is kinder to the woman. There is always a need for people who can relate well to others, who are sensitive to feelings and emotions. A woman does not necessarily lose this kind of 'employment' with age; while a man may find himself at a loss – no job to go to in the morning, and not much skill in the fine points of interpersonal relationships and expressive activities.

The woman, however, is apt to be more vulnerable through the death of her mate as she is likely to outlive him. This not only may be a source of much personal distress, but may at one blow place her apart from the rest of the society now that she is no longer half of a couple. However, even before her husband's death, she may have suffered a loss in status and social integration because of his retirement. Disengagement theory tells us that it is natural for distance between society and the individual to increase with advancing age. It is part of basic human development.

However, the process can be experienced with varying degrees of pain or satisfaction. The person who is pushed out by society before he is quite ready is likely to feel distress and will perhaps try vainly to push back. The man who can cultivate the social and expressive dimensions of his personality after retirement is more likely to enjoy his later years. The widow who is able to attain a new level of independence and self-reliance after her husband's death is more apt to be a successful disengager than the one who remains but a shadow of her former married self.

Many other researchers have looked into disengagement theory and have found that it does *not* hold up well as a firm general statement about how and why people age in the social sphere. A number of studies find that the active and engaged old person tends to have higher morale than the person who has withdrawn from the mainstream, and this is taken by some investigators as disproof of the theory's major implications.[3] The original propositions also did not give much attention to individual differences, and this has further weakened the case.

There is no denying, however, that some people do go through a sequence of diminishing social integration that fits the descriptions offered by disengagement theory. The idea that typical changes in our physical capacities and in our personal lifestyle interact with the society's need and bring about a change in established relationships cannot be rejected outright. Although disengagement theory does not apply as a general explanation, it includes concepts that ring true for the lives of many of us in contemporary society.

Pushing the old aside

There is a quality in the disengagement theory that one might almost call 'polite'. It emphasises that society and the individual take leave of each other with mutual consent. But other social scientists see the situation differently.[4] They agree with the broad conclusion drawn by disengagement theory: the old person tends to remove himself from the core of a society's life. However, they are more apt to use such terms as 'discrimination', 'segregation', and 'political expedience'. They do not see it as a gracious ritualistic dance. Society steers or pushes the old person to the sideline. Although disengagement does occur, they do not see it as a natural process. Instead it is society's solution to a variety of economic, social and political problems.

Age-grading (as explained in Chapter 1) has taken new forms in the twentieth century. In the past, young and old generally worked as they could on the many tasks that had to be done to keep family and community float. The young worked as early in life as they were able, and the old as long as they were able. It was biological capacity or functional status that determined when a person entered and departed from the work force. Today both young and old are increasingly excluded from the producer's role. The basic is not biological, for children and the aged are healthier and stronger than in the past. The basis is cultural; people are defined as 'too young' and 'too old' for longer periods of time than ever before.

Both the young and the old pushed out into a sort of social limbo. The demographers express this situation through their

Young and old together in an English hop-harvest, before modern age-barriers arrived.

term *'dependency ratio'*. It refers to the number of persons in the non-working years to each 100 persons in the working years. Currently this places both the 20-and-unders and the 65-and-overs among the non-workers. The dependency ratio in the USA is 86. In other words, for every 100 people drawing pay for their work, 86 others depend on them. The ratio of 'too young' to 'too old' in the non-worker group changes over time. Presently there are about three youths for every old person. In the years ahead, however, the balance will swing ever more heavily toward older dependants[5]

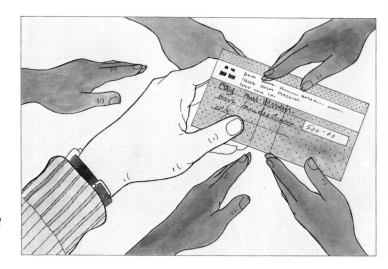

How many people depend on this single pay cheque each week?

Today, *stratification by age* has gained unusual importance. It is one more dividing line for people, and one more basis on which rights and privileges might be denied by the more powerful to the less powerful. Gregory Johnson and Lawrence Kamara even suggest that the middle-aged are at war with their juniors and seniors, rather than engaged in a decorous dance.

Competing generations

Education and retirement, of course, are spheres of activity to which people can be assigned when they are not welcome in the work force. Middle-aged people are able to enforce such assignments because they manoeuvre shifting age *coalitions*. Sometimes the middle-aged join with the old to exclude the young; at other times they are in collusion with the young to expel the old. The results of this power display by the middle-aged can be seen in economic discrimination, age stereotyping and territorial segregation. *Economic discrimination* shows up not only in employment, but also in barriers to obtaining credit, negligent or even criminal mishandling of pension plans, etc.

Historically power belonged to the old. Since World War II the middle-aged and young have become more powerful.

Age stereotyping is a way of rationalising the exclusion of young and old from positions of opportunity and power. The young may be dismissed as irresponsible and frivolous, the old as used-up and rigid. Looked at from this point of view, age stereotyping takes on a sinister character. More than just carelessness and insensitivity, it emerges as part of an unspoken policy of discrediting those who might be competitors for social power.

Although the term as such was not used, *territorial segregation* has been mentioned several times in this book. There is an increasing tendency for both the segregation of the aged (whether in miserable or handsome settings) and for the development of 'youth ghettos'. It is possible to identify more and more youth communities or old-age communities, which make it clear that neither is really part of the power élite. It is disturbing to think of our generations as warring with each other. It is not far-fetched theory, however, when social statistics are consulted; even our own daily observations can confirm it.

There is glow of constructive possibility here that seems to be absent with disengagement theory. If society has created definitions that set people apart from other, then society may also have the ability to redefine and integrate. There is more than one way to retain power, and sharing it is not necessarily the worst. As more people become *aware* of the power aspects of age-based exclusions, there may be more opportunity to develop alternatives. Young and old could stand together on more issues. The middle-aged would appreciate more keenly the benefits they might gain by allowing their juniors and seniors to shoulder part of the burden.

The problem of retirement

Is it necessary that our lives and our theories place so much emphasis on employment, productivity, earnings? Both the disengagement and conflict theories sketched here do give a lot of attention to the meaning of work. This is justifiable. The achievements and social status associated with occupation are major ingredients in the way we judge ourselves and others. When asked who we are, don't we often answer in terms of our work? As long as values associated with work remain dominant in our society, they are important for the old.

Ploughing days are over ... But work became sport for these men, who now rally their traction engines instead.

The barren thought that there really is no life worth mentioning after work has been disproved many times. Increasingly, studies of the retirement years reveal diversity of 'after lives'. Not all retirees stay retired. Many continue to be active in fields related to their life-long interests; other cultivate new interests or return to interests they could not find time for earlier. Some of the best students I know are elderly men and women.

Old interests take on new dimensions in retirement.

It is probable that values such as learning, self-discovery and helping other people will become regarded with as much respect as working and producing in the years to come. There are already signs that using time for pleasure and recreation is less accompanied by guilt than once was the case. This means that the middle-aged person immersed in his or her productive phase will not be in possession of all the truly 'valuable' values. Non-work activities will not be looked upon as merely marking time for the 'too-young' and 'too-old'. In fact, it is likely that middle-aged adults will begin demanding more opportunity to enjoy these activities themselves. This would, apart from advantages of its own, reduce the inter-generation conflict.

Age and personality

In this Greek village, men of all ages take part in an up-hill race in traditional costume.

The old person is largely responsible for his own place in society, to an extent that neither disengagement nor conflict theory emphasises enough. What is experienced as rejection or exclusion by one person may be welcome opportunity to shed responsibility by another. One individual's lifestyle may keep him closely linked with society, while that of another individual may encourage earlier disengagement.

The reality of individual differences was well illustrated by a study of *ageing and personality* conducted by Suzanne Reichard, Florine Livson and Paul Peterson.[6] They found five types of personality among the men in their study. In general, three types of men adjusted well to their place in society as they aged, while the other two types did not.

The '*rocking-chair*' men were of a passive disposition. Growing old gave them permission to withdraw from activities and responsibilities that they had not much cared for in the first place. What they gained in peace and quiet seemed to more than make up for what they lost by moving out of the mainstream. Quite different were the '*armoured* men'. These people dreaded the prospect of becoming passive, dependent or helpless. They organised themselves vigorously to resist all forces, both biological and sociological, that might place them in a dependent position. They maintained a physically and socially active lifestyle, hardly relinquishing their place in society at all.

The kind of personality most often seen among the well-adjusted elderly men was the one the researchers described as '*mature*'. They acknowledged the realities of ageing both in themselves and in their relationship with society. They were neither surprised nor embittered to find themselves growing old – it was just what they had expected. As people who had been living fully for many years, they had the confidence to continue to function well, enjoying personal relationships and their favourite activities. These were the three successful ways of finding a place in society.

Marbles for the boys, bowles for the men – street games make a thread through life for the French.

The 'angry' men showed the most common type of maladaptive pattern to ageing. These were people who felt they had not been treated well by life. With an overwhelming sense that they had somehow been cheated of life's pleasures and achievements, they moved into old age with complaints on their lips. Blaming others for their difficulties and refusing to acknowledge the encroachments of ageing were among the features in a lifestyle that made both themselves and others miserable.

The other poorly adjusting old men were described as the 'self-haters'. Like the angry men, these people came into old age with a sense of disappointment over their total lives. But they found the fault in themselves rather than others. These were the depressed men, having no use for the self they were growing old with.

Women and ageing

Although this particular study was limited to men, there is no reason to believe that individual differences among men and women are any less significant. The five types of personality noted by Reichard and her colleagues can also be seen in women. The place of the ageing woman in society has some distinctive elements as well as those shared with men. We can distinguish, for example, between the grown woman who continues to rely upon 'girlish charms', and the woman who develops new and deeper personality attributes that make her, in old age, a more

Masking the realities of ageing behind powder, paint and a wig.

impressive and powerful person than ever before. The fact that more young women are more active participants in the complete range of social activity and power-sharing strongly suggests that in old age their place will differ from that of their more 'protected' mothers who, throughout their lives, had been expected to limit themselves to a narrower realm.

Given a reasonable opportunity, people will find or create their own places in society as they grow old. The variety and depth of individual experience men and women bring into old age is a rich resource that society ignores only to its own disadvantage. The old person has helped to make society what it is and need not hestitate to make his or her claim to a meaningful place in it.

The erect back reveals a proudly independent spirit.

6 Disaster– or challenge?

To most people, Miss B was a dynamo, a whirlwind and an excellent source of gossip. The tiny old woman was here, there, and everywhere, making everybody's business her own. We were surprised, then, to find her alone, shuffling about with downcast eyes. Miss B, of all people, was depressed.

The family and friends of Mr W were concerned for another reason. Usually a quiet, reserved individual, he had become loud, restless and argumentative. He was taking offence at little things and, in general, being difficult. People did not know what to expect from him next.

These people were both experiencing some of the turbulence that can accompany the passage into and through old age. Their external reactions to the turbulence were obvious to all, but the stormy currents that had upset them in the first place were not so clear.

This chapter covers the problems that often threaten to disrupt the lives of old people, and with strategies for coping with these difficulties.

An inconvenience for one person may be a disaster for another. One person may accept a setback such as forced retirement or a hip fracture as a challenge, another may be completely demoralised. The individual who can bear up well against one source of threat or loss may be extremely vulnerable to some other problem, even if 'objectively' that other problem does not appear so important to an outsider.

Loss of security

An old person's sense of security can be undermined in many ways. It is not even necessary for anything terrible to happen – yet. The *anticipation* that one might lose something critical to the sense of basic security can in itself be very disturbing. One person, for example, may be used to having his opinions and wishes determine what happens in the family. Should the day

*What lies behind
Miss B's sudden
depression?*

come when people no longer obey – perhaps no longer even listen to – his proclamations, then he might well feel rather like a deposed monarch. His sense of security has derived from his ability to control or significantly influence the lives around him. Any intimation that this interpersonal control might be lost could be alarming. Any changes in the family hierarchy (even the possibility of change) may cause the person to feel insecure.

This is only one possible source of insecurity. Another person may be secure in the steady affection and support of one particular individual: 'If anything happened to ——, I wouldn't know what to do. I couldn't go on.' Still another might base the rock of security upon financial assets, a bit of money put away for property, the pension, the emergency, knowing that there are financial resources to meet current and future needs.

Careful attention must be given to the needs of the inhabitants when renewing or replacing old city areas.

For some people the sense of security is visible and palpable: the place they live in, the familiar furnishings, the neighbourhood, and, of course, the faces they see around them. They may not actually *enjoy* all this. There may be endless complaints about the poor heating, the noisy neighbours and so forth. But everything that contributes to the fabric of daily life also contributes to the basic sense of security. The person continues to know and value himself because the intimate world around him continues to affirm his identity.

Physical setbacks

The relationship between health and emotional security may also be critical, as has been confirmed by research.[1] Major illness and impairment can easily be understood as threats to security. However, physical setbacks that are not life-threatening in themselves can lay the foundation for psychological disaster.

An old person may have an episode of incontinence, for example. This can generate self-doubt, perhaps even shame. He or she becomes reluctant to participate in social life out of fear of embarrassment, even after the episode had passed. The person would rather withdraw from human relationships than face possible rejection, avoidance, pity or ridicule. The trigger need not be incontinence. It can be skin changes, problems with hearing or vision – anything that threatens to reduce the person's status and functioning in society.

Limitations on physical mobility may spell disaster for other old people. One who copes with stressful situations by taking himself elsewhere would be deprived of this defensive move. He is forced to remain within high-tension situations, perhaps beyond the point of his psychological endurance. He may become anxious to the extent of irrationality, or sink into a depressed withdrawal.

He may also be especially vulnerable to psycho-physiological suffering as shown, for example, by pathological changes in blood pressure, digestion, and cardiac functioning.

Becoming trapped

Some people have organised their basic sense of security around their sphere of work and activity. For them, the loss of employment is a threat because it closes an outlet for self-expression and constructive energy. The person can no longer define himself in terms of his occupation. 'I used to be a——' seems like a feeble self-definition when compared with 'I am a——'. Even the apprehension about loss of employment or other self-defining activity can be enough to precipitate inner crisis.

Living only for the new generations

The old should live with children, not through them.

There is one more possible threat to security. A person well past his 50's may be living as much through children and grandchildren as through his or her own direct experiences. He asks little

for himself, and illness, financial hardship and other adversities do not undermine his personal sense of security. However, should misfortune strike the younger generation, then his whole life crumbles. Concern that something might happen can also be a source of perturbation even when the skies appear blue and clear to everybody else.

It is easy to be glib and attribute an old person's depression or agitation to 'senility' or, just as carelessly, to 'old age'. But if we know the person and what is critical for his or her sense of basic emotional security, then we can appreciate the disturbed state of mind as a natural response to certain experienced threats. Of primary importance is the fact that the person himself experiences the threats as real.

Security equals dependency

A grim choice confronts some people when they face problems associated with advancing age. Do they have to accept insecurity and deprivation? Must they surrender much of their independence and integrity in order to be helped? Elderly men and women may prefer to go it alone instead of taking advantage of resources to which they are entitled. To the world they may appear as stubborn and unrealistic. But they feel that life would no longer be worth while if they were to become dependent on others for their needs.

A hard life at a natural pace makes for a long working life.

72

Young adults may already fear the dependency associated with old age. It is not unusual for them to declare that they would rather die than grow old. Thus, a dread of old age already influences the thoughts, feelings and actions of people who are still years away from it.

Since this fear of dependency weighs heavily upon so many people, both old and not-so-old, it is important to examine the psychological and bio-social realities.

Why does dependency appear such a grim prospect? We all began life as helpless infants dependent on others for our survival and well-being. It takes us years to reach the point where we can take major responsibility for our own lives. Many of the steps along the way are difficult, and few of us make our way without struggle and conflict. We have to prove our independence, to ourselves and others, and we have to overcome temptations to slide back to earlier stages of dependency.

We recognise the advantages of independence and the obstacles we have overcome to gain it. On the other hand, there are times when it seems so pleasant to drift into a more passive condition, seemingly to relinquish what we have achieved. Let somebody else take care of us, make the tough decisions, protect, nurture . . .

These retired Dutch fishermen deliberately keep old styles alive.

This common ambivalence is complicated by biological and cultural expectations and impulses. As adults we may be called upon not only to be self-reliant, but also to meet the dependency needs of others, especially young children. This can be especially

The sidewalk artist's drawing is his statement of independence.

hard on the type of person who has strong dependency cravings beneath a façade of independence.

Society expects us to behave like grown-ups. Thus we impersonate independent adults much of the time, while in our heart of hearts we would prefer to be babied ourselves. The pressure may be most relentless upon men. In many cultures it is considered unmanly to show any feelings of uncertainty, grief or tenderness, let alone the open need to be loved or comforted. The more extreme our fixation on independence, the more threatening the prospect of dependency.[2]

Biologists and social gerontologists are more objective about dependency. They point out that there is nothing shameful about the dependency of the baby and young child. They need to be cared for to ensure survival and promote development.

In the same way, certain dependencies are naturally associated with old age. An old person is not a baby by any means, but it is normal for the old to need help and protection as their physical resources diminish. There is nothing inherently wrong or shameful about this situation.

The burden of bureaucracy

Fear of dependency in old age is heightened by bureaucratic procedures and dismal social attitudes. The person who has cultivated a lifestyle around intimate human relationships and a certain amount of privacy may be threatened by the complexity and impersonality of the 'establishment' that has the means to provide help. He is acutely sensitive of becoming a number and being asked nosey questions.

Today's old people grew up in an age when mutual aid was the primary source of assistance. Family, friends, neighbours came to each other's rescue with whatever resources they had. To them, turning to bureaucratic establishments may seem peculiar, even an admission of defeat and rejection. The younger generation today, on the other hand, has many decades to interact with 'the establishment' or 'the system,' and so will be more prepared for this form of help in old age.

Inner conflicts

It is easy to understand the terror a person may experience in the midst of a flood or a fire, or an earthquake. We are ready to come to his rescue, and are not surprised if he seems, for the moment, psychologically devasted. Yet there may be panic of a very private nature that is just as well justified. An old person may sense that his life is falling apart as surely as buildings crumble in an earthquake. The sense of *disintegration* sometimes emerges from inner conflicts, not that visible to the outsider. The person himself may be unable to put his feelings into words, and people may not listen carefully to the words he *does* use. The sense of disintegration can have many causes, for example the premonition of death.

Recognising the signs

The suffering of old people is sometimes unrecognised because we assume it is natural for this to be a time of low spirits. We often mistake an old person's quiet withdrawal and lack of complaint as philosophic acceptance when, in fact, he is putting the best possible face on a bitterly disappointing, humiliating or frightening situation.

Either assumption – that it is normal to be unhappy or that old people are somehow happy about being unhappy – obstructs our view of the person's true state of mind. Signs of distress deserve attention in old age as much as at any point in the lifespan.

Depression is one of the most common expressions of emotional distress in old men and women. The basic symptoms of depression are similar throughout adult life, but in old age it can be difficult to know where a physical difficulty leaves off and depression begins.

Reduced appetite and inability to get a good night's sleep, for example, are among the clues that suggest depression. But old people may choose to eat less and have sleep difficulties for reasons other than depression. It is when an entire pattern begins to emerge that we should seriously consider the possibility of a depressive reaction.

The pattern is likely to include reduced and slowed-down speech, the person may seem to be thinking slower as well. There is less attention to personal grooming. Energy is lacking even for routine activities. A general feeling of pessimism prevails and life appears increasingly grim and hopeless.

There may be talk of feeling empty inside, and of being a useless, worthless person. The future holds nothing; the past is no source of comfort; the present moment is intolerable. The depressed person usually turns his feelings against himself, sometimes he also lashes out in anger at other people.

In such a condition there is a heightened risk to survival. Suicide is one possibility – and the suicide rate in old age is high, especially in white males. But there are also other ways in which the old, depressed person may endanger his own life. He may neglect a medical regime that is necessary to control an illness such as diabetes. He may limit himself to bed and chair, becoming increasingly inactive and thus more vulnerable to degenerative processes and infections. Unsociable behaviour, often characteristic of depression, may also drive away the people who would otherwise shield him from a number of life-threatening circumstances. Depression may also be misinterpreted as proof of senility, causing further social isolation and incorrect treatment.

Mistaken symptoms

The perturbed old person may have other symptoms either along with or in alternation with depression. He may be agitated, confused, paranoid, go through episodes of keyed-up manic behaviour. Some people express their symptoms indirectly through physical complaints, intensifying existing physical problems and developing new problems by emotional upset. It requires a wise person as well as a competent doctor to respond to the true distress that is represented by the mixture of psychological and physical symptoms.

The intimate connection between psychological and physical distress in the elderly can reveal itself in many ways. An episode of mental confusion, for example, might be misinterpreted as 'just old age', 'going a little crazy', or being upset about some personal situation. In fact, it may instead be a symptom of a myocardial infarction or congestive heart failure. Emotional distress and mental confusion in old age can be, at the same time, a response to psychosocial problems and to serious physical disease processes.

Confusion in the mind can be a sign of a physical problem, rather than mental decline.

This is also true for a symptom known as 'regression'. Regressive thought and behaviour is seen more often in old age than at any other time. It has unusual power to alarm and dismay the observer. A polite and proper old person suddenly treats his friends to a virtuoso display of obscenities. Another displays a childish quality of thought and action that does not seem appropriate to the situation.

Progressive deteriorative processes in the central nervous system can be involved. But it could be a sign that the old person's resources have been temporarily overtaxed by emotional stress. Adult behaviour does not seem to work, and there is not enough psychological energy to keep strong needs and impulses under their usual social control, so that they break out into open expression, carrying some shock value with them.

We have seen many people pass through such episodes and return to a successful adult level of functioning.

Answering distress

No single principle of mental health can guarantee that a person will pass through the challenges and perils of a long life without experiencing distress. Loss, suffering and human error are part of most lives. However, it is within our abilities to reduce the depth and frequency of suffering and to help each other when our own resources are temporarily overrun.

In old age distress can be more acute since immediate problems bring to mind earlier difficulties. The old person may be haunted by memories of stressful events and relationships as far back as early childhood. Tormented by both past and present, he may feel helpless. At the same time, there may be fewer resources available to cope with problems in the immediate situation – fewer people to share experiences with, less physical and financial control over the environment, and so on.

Treating distress – conventionally and unconventionally.

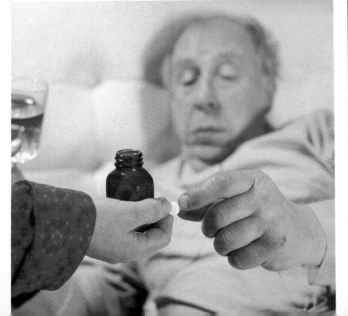
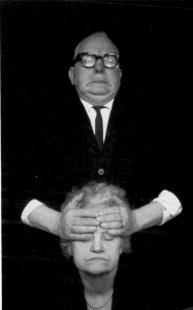

With support and appropriate treatment, Miss B is back to her brisk and active self.

We can help such a person by encouraging him to use all the control he still has, and by supporting him in all his remaining areas of vigour and competence. We can hear him out, listening carefully to his sorrows and alarms. This sharing is not only useful in itself, but it can also help the old person to realise that problems of the past need not continue to weigh upon him today.

We can help each other by giving support and security without asking a high psychological price for it. An impaired or emotionally upset old person should be helped without asking for anything in return and without unnecessary invasion of privacy. We should not assault a person's integrity, condescend to him, or deprive him of rights in the name of welfare.

Old people who face difficult life situations or have inner emotional problems benefit from psychological consultations. However, this possibility seldom suggests itself to them, for many grew up in the pre-psychotherapy era. It must also be said that there are still relatively few counsellors and therapists who appreciate the contribution they could make in this area. For many years it was assumed that old people were not appropriate candidates for therapy. Fortunately, however, some clinicians have opened themselves to this challenge and discovered that psychotherapy can prove effective with the old as well as the young.[3] It is to be hoped that individual and group therapy will become increasingly available and acceptable to the elderly.

There is general agreement that there is a higher percentage of people suffering emotional distress in old age than at any other time in adult life. Yet the provision of mental health services for the elderly is much below the average.[4] The gap between need and suitable care is all too often filled by dubious measures, such as heavy-handed prescription of drugs.

Two problems – two solutions

Miss B and Mr W, in the introductory paragraph to this chapter, expressed their distress differently. Yet both had shown a change from previous ways of thinking and feeling. To learn what was troubling Miss B all one had to do was ask her. She was forthright in her reply: 'Ninety! *Ninety!*'

Miss B explained that she would be turning 90 in a few days and this, of course, meant that she would be old. Old and washed up. Old and useless. Old and everything terrible. Although this attitude might have struck an outsider as peculiar, the difference between 89 and 90 was psychologically as significant to Miss B as, say, the transition between 29 and 30 or 39 and 40 might be to another person. With some support and a reminder of how many challenges she had already mastered in her life, Miss B agreed that she could at least wait and see what harm being 90 might bring to her. A few weeks later (and older), Miss B was back to her usual brisk and active self.

Mr W's problem proved more complex and serious. He was afraid that he was going to be eased out of the household and put into a nursing home. This fear was constructed from little pieces of reality, some misunderstandings, and a general sense of distress with signs of ageing. He felt himself in a battle for survival. Like a warrior with his back to the wall he tried to frighten or beat off his attackers: thus his uncharacteristic loud, pushy, argumentative behaviour, his over-protestation of vigour and power. Fortunately the crisis point was never reached.

A person respected by everyone in the family helped to create a climate of improved communication. As the family members expressed their true thoughts and feelings (instead of having to make guesses about everybody else's intentions), the tension drained away. Nobody really wanted Mr W out of the way – far from it! With no more sense of attack, there was no more need for the sort of defence that had been puzzling and upsetting the family.

'Good company is the best doctor.'

79

'Isn't life
beautiful?'
'All the more so
with you dear.'

80

7 Love and intimacy in later life

'You're looking pretty tonight.' Her eyes warm to the compliment. Automatically she checks her hair, newly washed and cut. Even after all these years she is still slightly nervous. But a date is still a date, even when you are seventy-and-more. For his part, any tentative feelings are covered with pride and pleasure at being seen out with such a fine woman – much as he felt fifty years and more ago. 'Shall we go?'

A lifetime of loving

Every old person has his own, individual life story. For the old, there may well be new pleasures and sorrows to come. But these relate to the entire shape of their lives, not simply to the status of being old. This applies as much to loving and intimacy as to anything else in old age.

Nonetheless, the sexual thoughts, feelings and actions of an old person are best understood from a broader perspective than those of a younger person. It would be wrong to reduce the wealth of anyone's experience in these fields to a statistical chart of 'how often's'. Who has this person been? What is the overall nature and quality of life now? How does this person's sexuality relate to his or her entire lifestyle?

The cradle is not too early a place to seek the roots of what eventually will flower into the loving relationships of mature adults. One baby receives affection and attention from the time it enters the family constellation. A basic feeling that 'I am lovable' develops easily in such a circumstance. There is abundant opportunity to learn how to relate and share affection with others. Another baby enters a family that does not have much affection to offer. This child may have a more difficult challenge ahead. In later life this may be the person who finds it difficult to believe anybody really cares for him.

The old person who easily gives and receives affection and the one whose emotional insecurity leads to constant demands for reassurance may have taken their divergent paths in early childhood. The love we give to infants and children today is likely to radiate back to family and society, as well-nurtured seedlings bear fruit beyond our own harvestings.

Sexual coming-of-age

Another critical period is adolescence and early adulthood. By this time, the individual has had the opportunity to develop many relationships. Now there is the new challenge of functioning as a sexually mature being. There are conquests, pleasures and adventures, as well as the insecurities, disappointments and the thwarted adventures that many experience in their sexual coming-of-age. These contribute significantly to the state of mind with which the individual approaches intimate relationships in old age. Some people bring with them confidence in their ability to love and be loved; others remain burdened by anxieties that stem from painful disappointments in early childhood.

Stressful situations in later years once again question the individual's sexual desirability and competence. The circumstances are different, but the basic challenge may be the same as many years before, when the person had to prove him or herself for the first time. Thus it is the person who has known success in the past who is most likely to remain open for loving intimacy in later years. A couple with a mutual history of strong physical affection is likely to share more caresses in old age than a middle-aged couple who have already grown out of the habit of touching each other.

Active young lovers – active old lovers

Studies of sexual activity and interest in old people confirm that active young lovers are more likely to become active old lovers.[1] A man or woman who has enjoyed sexual intimacies for years is likely to continue an active love life. However, most research

At ease with himself and still able to charm.

does suggest a general decline in the amount of sexual interest and activity with age.

But how important is the frequency of sexual contact? In old age, meanings and numbers have rather little to do with each other. Each sexual union between a long-devoted couple is an affirmation that goes beyond the pleasure of the moment. Years of love imbue the occasion. If it is just one contact this month, this may nevertheless be a contact that renews three, four, or five decades of intimacy. Each partner keeps the sense of being desirable and the identity of a sexually alive person. The satisfaction and meaning of such an experience must escape those who have never had an enduring relationship.

And this survival of sensual awareness tends to make the person more vital and attractive in many interpersonal relationships, not just the overtly sexual. Staying sexually alive is one way of avoiding the drabness sometimes associated with old age.

Inhibitions and obstacles

Once interrupted by illness or infirmity, sexual functioning may not rebound easily. Poor health can cause a reduction or suspension of sexual activity at any age. He or she must contend with the accumulated effect of infirmities suffered through the years, as well as new problems. There is also a tendency for many of the ailments of later life to become chronic. The old person learns to live with discomfort and limitation. Yet this is only part of the difficulty. Some physical problems develop or become chronic because they are not treated promptly and effectively.

Barriers raised by doubt and fear
The poor health of one partner usually means that *both* are deprived of sexual expression. An interruption of this kind in later life can raise doubts in both minds. It may not be entirely clear, for example, whether it is disability or a loss of interest that has curtailed sexual contact. 'Perhaps I'm not appealing to him any more,' the wife may wonder, as old doubts return. This is a fairly common worry, because many men in our society feel they have to minimise the extent of physical illness. The woman may then be left wondering precisely why their life together has changed so disturbingly.

Each person can become trapped and isolated in personal fear and self-protective strategies. An ill husband may fend off his wife's display of affection because he thinks he will be unable to match up to the sexual performance that is expected. The doubts, rebuffs and miscommunications may persist even if his physical condition improves. The healthy partner may conclude prematurely that their sex life together has come to an end. This attitude can interfere with possible renewal of the sexual relationship even if the ailing partner recovers.

The chaste widow?

One of the most powerful barriers to loving intimacy in old age is the permanent loss of a partner through death. It may be a long time before the bereaved husband or wife thinks again of another relationship. Some never do. Even those who eventually experience again the yearning for a close relationship may feel loyalty to the dead spouse, and perhaps a sense of discomfort in 'looking around' again after so many years of married life.

There is a marked difference here between the responses of bereaved men and women. Widowers are more likely than widows to remarry. The woman, however, is more likely to be the marital survivor in the first place, for two main reasons. The mortality rate for males is greater at every age level, from infancy onward, and secondly, our culture encourages men to marry women somewhat younger than themselves.[2]

We still live in a society that expects women to remain the prim and passive objects of male pursuit. This certainly complicates the woman's quest for a new relationship. For a start, there are relatively few available men around (and those that are seem still to seek younger women). It is also not considered quite respectable for the elderly woman with her long experience of loving to take the initiative.

A setting for romance

Travel agencies try to persuade us that romance flourishes in the right setting. Advertisements barrage us with products that promise to make us sexy, glittering, powerful, desirable.

Although these messages are biased and superficial, they do touch the truth. There are circumstances that quicken our heartbeat and sharpen our appreciation for sensual possibilities. We feel good and we want to share this feeling. We look good to each other and something very pleasant might well happen.

Unfortunately, the general lifestyles of many old people are a long way from anyone's romantic ideal. Their immediate physical environment, the clothes they wear, the activities they can share together – many of the elements that contribute to the 'feel' of daily life – are often limited by finances. Even basic requirements may be lacking.

The old man may lack the hearing aid that would help natural intimate dialogue; the old woman may be wearing glasses that have needed replacing for a long time. He might feel more like a live man if he had a smart addition to his wardrobe and the means to take his wife somewhere special. She might feel more special herself if she could afford a beauty treatment now and then. Both might feel more ready for sexual intimacy if they lived in a less noisy and dingy neighbourhood. Lusty, healthy young adults can more easily overcome the distractions, inconveniences and even ugliness that may surround them. Nonetheless most young lovers will prefer certain settings that make them feel 'right'. And old lovers could benefit even more from an environment conducive to ease, stimulation and pleasure.

Couldn't or shouldn't?

It has been said that the largest sexual organ is the brain. Physical excitement, performance and enjoyment follow naturally when we think ourselves into passion. By the same token, the physical side of loving can be disconnected through a negative mental state. It is most likely that the major barriers to sexual intimacy in later life are to be found in the mind. Many of us assume that old people *do not* have much of a sex life. Why? Because they *cannot*. But if they could? Well, then, they shouldn't! This is a tangle of half-truth, attitude, and value judgement. Let us first examine the facts, and then our attitudes and values.

We have already mentioned a number of factors that make it difficult for people to maintain sexual relationships with advancing age. Despite these problems, however, researchers agree that sexual interest and activity are important at every age. We do not cease as sexual beings at the age of 50, 65, 75, and advanced age does not mean the end of sexuality.[3]

To maintain a sexual relationship, the elderly couple must overcome strong expectations and admonitions to the contrary. The attitudes of society affect men and women somewhat differently for both biological and psychosocial reasons.

'Quick look and see if I've dropped a stitch!'

Men seem to reach their peak in sheer virility during late adolescence and early adulthood. The decline generally begins long before old age. The middle-aged man has already tapered off appreciably, both in the number of orgasms and in the intervals between them. There comes a time when the ageing male may face the social stigma of being a 'dirty old man' if he continues an obvious interest in sexuality.

Fear of ridicule and disapproval can fill sexual love with conflict. The combination of social pressure with gradual biological decline can result in impotence. The elderly man wants the respect of society and the respect of his own conscience. To maintain this respect he may relinquish an active sex life, either through conscious decision or through impotence.

Each one to his own taste.

I remember a long conversation with a man of 93. He lived in a medical institution that was more of a home than a hospital for him, although he had health problems that required close monitoring. Winds of scandal were swirling about him. There had been talk about Mr B and one of the younger women in the institute. Then there had been a celebrated occasion when he was said to have propositioned a female staff member. Now, to top it all, there were persistent rumours that he had been 'involved' with one of the volunteer workers and was planning to make her the third Mrs B.

Mr B still liked women; always had. But, 'It's been getting so that every time I'm with a woman I wonder, "Is this going to be the *last* time?" He was grateful for every pleasure that still came his way in life, including the intimacy of sexual relations.

'When that light goes out in my eyes – if it ever goes out – then I won't think as much of myself. And neither will anybody else. I think I would just be dead on my feet, like some of the people you see around here... But when a fellow my age *does* have something going, well, you know how people talk around here. I'm a wicked, wicked man, or some sort of clown to them.'

The large, well-built man with a gentle face and sparse silver hair paused a moment. Then he raised both fists to punctuate his conclusion: 'I'm damned if I *do* and I'm damned if I *don't!*' To the people around Mr B, he had become a 'disturbing influence' although he was simply following the lifestyle he had established many decades ago. At some invisible point in time, society had decide that his romantic life was supposed to cease. The pressure on Mr B was especially acute because he lived in an institution. Sexual relationships and any type of strong interpersonal bonds between residents are observed and evaluated in a way that most of us would find unacceptable in our private lives. The difficulty in maintaining a private life in an institution setting creates yet another barrier to loving intimacy.

She's just won a legs competition; he's had a winning lap all his life.

Pressure is also often felt by old men living in other circumstances. Family and neighbours sometimes act as though the intimate relationships of an old man need their approval. Their grown children may behave as though the old person were in fact an inexperienced, impulsive youth who could embarrass them by 'doing something foolish', such as falling in love or sprucing up as a candidate for romance.

Many an elderly man has been told to his face that he was 'too old for that sort of thing'. Others have heard the condescending laughter and the jests that are so popular in this subject. It is easy to surrender to the subtle and not so subtle pressures and declare oneself no longer a sexual being.

The ageing woman's situation is also complicated by the interaction between her psychobiological status and the social climate.[4] Unlike men, the 'average' woman becomes even more sexually responsive after adolescence. Instead of beginning a decline as early as the 20s, the woman tends to bloom more fully in her 30s and 40s. Women who keep their mates and their health are quite able to enjoy an active sex life through all the years that remain to them.

One study has found that 70 per-cent of women over the age of 60 engage in sexual intercourse with their husbands, despite all the barriers mentioned. This says something for the strength of the romantic bonds between men and women.

Two victims of one image

Unfortunately, however, the preservation of sexual intimacy for the elderly woman is obstructed by negative attitudes and values, some indirect, but nevertheless powerful. Old men who bow to social expectations and pressures by relinquishing their sexual activity leave their women without physical love as well. The 'dirty old man' image claims two victims.

Consider one fairly typical pattern. The woman has become relatively free from the everyday demands of raising young children. She has more time and energy to devote to herself and her husband. 'I'm ready to have a life of my own' she says. She is more relaxed and secure as a person than she was at the start of her lovelife many years before. Physically and emotionally, she may be ready to flourish as a sexually loving partner.

But what is happening in her husband's life at this time? He may be at the peak of involvement with his career. Responsibilities and concerns about work and financial status may demand much attention. His self-esteem centres around his standing and his prospects in his work, and his ability to provide financially for the future.

The marital relationship may be taken for granted, perhaps have grown a little stale. The woman who has been sharing his life is seen as a mother to the children and as a companion. He

Living together – but apart in many ways.

may have lost touch with her sensitivities as a person and, especially, with her continuing potential for sexual vibrancy. He experiences a gradual decline in his own psychosexual drive and may react in various ways, often including efforts to reassure himself through 'new quests' or other means.

The man is also quick to assume that his wife's interest in sexuality has been ebbing. In our society it is difficult for a man to face the possibility that his woman is at least his equal in sexual interest; for so much of his life he has been persuaded that he is the aggressive initiator.

Displays of romantic interest and passion on the part of his wife may now be threatening. They seem to reverse the natural order of things. Marriage counsellors have become increasingly familiar with the middle-aged man who has been 'scared off' and confused by his wife's sexuality at the very time that his virility has come, in his own mind at least, into question. This is when hope of a fulfilling love life in old age can be abandoned.

Some women in this situation try to keep their feelings to themselves. They fear that open expression of sexual interest will disturb their husband and create problems in the total relationship. They may also be burdened with negative attitudes absorbed from society.

The need to adapt

The woman often has lingering doubts about whether a 'good' person should have strong sexual needs. Sex is acceptable if it is for purposes of reproduction, or to meet her husband's needs. But *for herself*? Even if she is fairly 'liberated', she may not be entirely able to free herself of doubts.

Hardened attitudes inhibit the ageing man and woman as they reach out for each other. In a traditionally oriented couple, it is the husband who usually takes the lead. Once he becomes sexually aroused, his impulse is to move directly to intercourse. The woman has a different pattern of responding. Affection by word and touch is important for her to get into the mood. Foreplay arouses her more fully, and she values continued intimacy after the act of intercourse. If her husband lacks sensitivity to her feelings, or control over his own behaviour, then the experience could fall short of fulfillment, but even so, love-making may be pleasurable for the woman. She is reassured of her husband's interest and the relationship is kept alive.

This long-standing pattern of love-making may no longer work with the husband and wife's changing psychobiological status. If both partners are convinced that sexual contact should consist of a wink, pinch, and a quick drive toward orgasm, they will not be accustomed to the mood-setting, fondling, the spontaneous and uninhibited actions that can arouse and satisfy. If they have become skilful lovers together, and learnt how to enjoy pleasing each other, modifying their basic impulses, and exploring a variety of sexual delights, then the relaxed couple with good mutual communication may naturally compensate for the change in status.

Doorways and pubs are traditional meeting places the world over.

The attitude that 'We can't and we shouldn't' tends to become a self-fulfilling prophecy. At the very least, it adds a note of anxiety and pressure into one of our most intimate forms of relationship. As men and women surrender their sexual sides, they may move apart in other ways.

The triumph of love

Despite the obstacles, love can triumph for the old as well as for the young. The importance of a sustained love relationship in old age is hard to overestimate. Sex brings more than direct physical gratification, although this itself is not to be slighted. It also reaffirms each partner's identity as a person who can offer something worthwhile, who can *be* someone worthwhile to another person. The body is still a means of giving and receiving pleasure. Old lovers like their bodies better than those who have closed this chapter in their lives.

But there is another important function of sexual intimacy in old age. The old person is all too often 'type-cast' to the outside world. He is the secondary character, belonging on the fringe of the real action. We tend to remain at an emotional distance from him. Every day we walk past, almost *through*, old people on the street, without clearly registering their existence as individuals.

How and where is the old person to find reassurance that he is truly an individual? That his distinctive personality has not been forgotten? That he means something to somebody? Surely, he cannot rely entirely on the sad image of himself that is reflected back to him by society.

The intimacy of two people who shared years, joys and sorrows together is an excellent buffer against a world that looks at old men and women but does not really see them. In each other's arms, they continue to be themselves rather than society's impoverished image of the aged. The small intimacies, the quiet conversation, the sense of togetherness remain both precious and life-affirming.

In years to come old lovers may have more of a chance than they do today. Society may come to recognise that oppressive attitudes toward sexual intimacy in old age merely reflect its own insecurities and misconceptions.

If we expect to remain sexually alive beyond early adulthood, then we are likely to do so. And if we can overcome unexamined prejudices against those suspected of being old lovers today, then we are more likely to raise a new generation who will understand our own intimate relationships when we are old.

The triumph of enduring love.

8 The shadow of senility

Most of us feel helpless and heartbroken in the presence of an individual who has lost so much of what we associate with being an intact person. It is difficult to find ourselves unrecognised or ignored by a person we have loved and respected or to see him weep or rage for reasons that escape us. The fear of senility is a very real one, for it is a condition that can profoundly damage the victim and distress family, friends and those looking after him.

A minority problem?

The word 'senile' is used by physicians and gerontologists in connection with a cluster of genuine brain diseases and disorders. Senile dementia and senile psychosis, too, are regarded by some physicians and psychologists as separate conditions, while others believe that senile brain disease is one basic disorder that simply shows up in a variety of symptoms, or patterns of symptoms, depending upon the individual and the circumstances of his life.

What are the characteristics of the kind of old person whom most clinicians would consider 'senile'? Among the most obvious are those in the realm of thought. For example, the senile person tends to repeat the same statements over and over again. This is known as perseveration, and is closely related to several other cognitive problems. These include a lack of ideas and a slowed-down tempo of thought.

One of man's most valuable assets is his ability to develop and grasp abstractions. In normal mental health we can see the forest as well as the trees, understand subtle relationships, perform mathematical and logical operations, and come up with new ideas when confronted with new challenges. The person who is accurately classified as senile has often lost this type of cognitive ability.

He thinks concretely. In other words, he misses the relationships and implications that both give richer meaning to experience and help to solve problems. If, for example, he is asked how an apple and an orange are alike, he may reply, 'Oranges don't grow around here,' and then repeat this answer several times.

If the hospital crops your hair, you can always grow your beard to make up. The old, like everyone else, should not be judged by appearances.

Nevertheless, even with such a marked impairment in abstract thinking a person may still be accurate and sensible, though able to focus only on one detail at a time. For example, 'Oranges do not grow around here' may remain an accurate statement, even though it fails to answer the question.

Senility may also include serious difficulties with memory. The memory impairment is greatest for recent events. Yesterday may draw a blank. The person may not even recall something that happened ten minutes ago. Problems with memory are also experienced by many people who are old but not senile, but memory loss is more radical and extensive in senility. Isolated memories may remain accessible, but the memory is lost as a general resource for coping with life.

Another very important problem is that of lack of attention. The senile person does not pay attention well. The alertness and concentration needed to register new experience seems to be missing or undependable. He may not remember what you said a moment ago, because he could or did not summon the kind of sustained attention necessary for the information to take hold in his mind in the first place.

So it is not surprising that the senile person often has great difficulty in coping with even the routine tasks and challenges of life, let alone with situations that arouse special anxiety or make special demands. Senility may therefore show itself in behaviour as well as thought. The senile individual may withdraw from interaction with others, have difficulty in keeping himself clean and groomed, suffer accidents related to forgetfulness or misunderstanding, and so on. Because his mental world has, in a sense, shrunk, the senile person can be severely handicapped in thought, behaviour and in encounters with other people.

Changes in the body

What physical changes in the central nervous system can contribute to the clinical picture of senility? Cerebral arteriosclerosis involves the hardening and narrowing of blood vessels that serve the brain. The resulting inadequate supply of nutrients and oxygen leads to deterioration of the afflicted brain cells. Those parts of the brain where the blockage of blood supply has been particularly impaired may atrophy and die, although other areas of the brain will continue to function fully.[1]

This process begins as early as the age of 50 in some individuals, although it is more likely to be detected in the mid-60s or beyond. Men appear to be somewhat more vulnerable to cerebral arteriosclerosis, for reasons that have yet to be determined. The explanation for the development of cerebral arteriosclerosis has not yet been established. Heredity, environmental pollution and cholesterol are among the influences that have been suggested.

Other common vascular problems involving blood supply include so-called 'little strokes', which produce temporary confusion, dizziness and nausea. Although the symptoms may subside, there is often remaining damage. Ischemic attacks (temporary reduction of oxygen supply to the brain) can also have lasting effects, although the person improves to some extent after the episode. The effects tend to show up in a fitful and episodic pattern, rather than a steady, predictable loss of function.

There is another common pattern of deterioration associated with old age, which is known as senile dementia. The most striking feature here is the widespread atrophy – that is, wasting away – of cells in the cerebral cortex, as distinguished from the here-and-there effects of cerebral arteriosclerosis. Furthermore, the damage occurs independent of change in the blood vessels.

The cause is unknown. Hereditary factors probably play some role, but some investigators believe that personality and environment also contribute. Research on this topic poses enormous challenges. The human brain still has its mysteries, despite years of ingenious observation and experimentation.

Arteriosclerosis and senile dementia, the two most common patterns of senile brain disease, show some difference in their effects on behaviour and in the courses they run.[2] Senile dementia usually expresses itself in the form of steady and gradual deterioration. The severe mental disorder, or psychosis, associated with cerebral arteriosclerosis shows a less predictable course. There may be periods of fairly good functioning, followed by sharp declines. Where the problems are to do with the function of blood vessels in the brain, the individual is more likely to retain some areas of clear memory and to function like his old self at times. However, it is not always easy in practice to determine the type of underlying brain pathology from thought and behaviour observations, especially when impairment is severe.

Unfortunately, these two general types of brain damage are progressive and, at present, not much can be done in terms of treatment or cures. There is no known way to repair structural damage to the brain, or to induce the body to do so. Both types of senile brain disease progressively disable the afflicted and also shorten their lives.

The danger in the label

Far too often, labelling a person 'senile' is a careless and ignorant expression, steeped in prejudice. Diagnosing a person as 'senile' is accurate only when we mean the pattern of progressively deteriorating thought and behaviour associated with irreversible brain damage. Careless use of this single word suggests that we think we know what is wrong, that there is nothing more to understand, or to be done. This attitude is not justified even when the person is, in fact, suffering progressive brain disease, as we shall see. But the attitude is particularly destructive when the person is troubled, yet far from 'senile'.

Even professionals are capable of making such errors. An international mental-health team found that many elderly patients are diagnosed as suffering from organic brain disease when their problems are actually functional.[3] If this can happen, then people without professional or scientific training may be even more prone to error. Any sign of confusion or mental lapse in an elderly person may be taken as 'proof' of senility. Let us examine some alternative explanations for 'senile' thought and behaviour.

Common mistakes

Few of us are at our best mentally when our bodies are beset by illness, distress or fatigue. We tend to be more charitable to ourselves than we are to old people ('I'm not feeling well, he is senile'). Yet many so-called 'senile' qualities of thought and behaviour are associated with states of poor health little different from our own.

Malnutrition is a common cause, whether from a bad or an inadequate diet. The old person may be suffering from chronic tiredness, related either to one of many possible illnesses, or to worry, depression and fearfulness. The prolonged deprivation of sleep can affect both behaviour and proper functioning of the mind in all of us. Physical disorders such as heart or kidney illness may upset metabolism and normal body rhythms, or result in the accumulation of toxic body products.

Poor health and senility are not one and the same.

Medical treatment can itself have adverse effects on an individual's performance. Drugs administered to treat a physical condition may result in a measure of drowsiness, agitation or confusion. Tranquillisers and anti-depressants may overshoot their intended effect or even, paradoxically, cause greater tension and agitation. The effects of any anesthesia may also be prolonged and disruptive to older people. In general, a person who is old has a low tolerance for drugs.

Judicious changes

Apart from the relatively direct impact of illness and treatment on the mental state of old people, the psychosocial effects of hospitalisation can also prove disturbing. An individual who has always been a rather private person and who now finds himself among strangers in a hospital ward may withdraw socially and lose some contact with the world around him. If treatment is carried out in a way that strips him of his identity and self-respect, this too can precipitate a mental flight that closely resembles senility. Confusion, unusual memory lapses, lethargy and related mental states can be important clues to physical disorders. A person may not be just senile, but disordered in thought and behaviour because of undetected or poorly treated illness. And unless measures are taken to diagnose and treat the

underlying physical disorder it may indeed lead to senility or to rapid death.

Frequently the signs of senility disappear rapidly when the physical problem has been attended to. Physicians who are sensitive to the needs of old men and women are often able to restore mental as well as physical health by judicious changes in diet and medication. Many times I have had the pleasure of talking with an alert, recuperating old person who a few days previously had been admitted to a geriatric hospital apparently hopelessly senile.

The effects of anxiety

A person who appears senile may be tormented by grief and anxiety. His 'demented' behaviour may have been brought about by emotional pain. A grieving person at any age is less able to pay close attention to everything that happens around him. He takes less care in grooming and dress. He has less emotional energy to welcome new opportunities or to respond to challenges. He may feel uncomfortable with his body. His mind may be constantly uneasy or tortured.

Loss and grief are common in old age as death removes loved ones. An old person may have suffered other significant losses, of occupation, residence, physical mobility, belonging, usefulness, all of which produce a grief response. So much mental and emotional energy may be absorbed by the multiple losses experienced by an old person that he drifts away from contact with the practical, daily environment. Add to this situation our own tendency to avoid the old and troubled, and we have a person left to dwell in sorrow.

Anxiety is another obstruction to clear mental functioning. When we are tense, frightened or insecure we are not likely to have firm control of our thoughts. We pay too much attention here, not enough there. We are so apprehensive that we cannot readily gather our ideas into concentrated focus, or shift to another topic when appropriate. We may become either too concrete or too abstract, depending upon our personality style. Our behaviour may become as fragmented as our thinking: restless pacing, doing and re-doing, fluttering, tapping, exercising our own brand of nervous habits. Or we may be paralysed by anxiety, unable to move our thoughts at all, rigid and automatic in our actions. Anxiety often makes intelligent people seem stupid.

Old people have good cause to be anxious. There are practical reasons: money, health, physical safety. There are psychological (which does not mean impractical) reasons as well. People bring anxieties and sorrows with them into old age, in addition to the new difficulties they encounter. The combination of old and new anxieties and sorrows may overtax the individual's ordinary coping abilities. Anxiety can be relieved, sorrow can be shared and as a result much of the senility can disappear, vanish. Constructive human relationships and a suitable environment can go a long way toward the prevention or reversal of mental changes that are too often mistaken for 'senility'.[4]

Senility as strategy

An old woman is sent into an institution, supposedly senile and uncommunicative. She doesn't speak and she doesn't understand (poor thing!). However, it soon becomes clear that she does speak and she does understand. Silence had been her way of punishing a family she regarded as cruel and insensitive. 'They're all living in my house and they treat me like a poor relation. Boss me around all the time!'

Her thoughts and opinions were not respected so she reached for a mental weapon that she knew could make her adversaries uncomfortable: silence. In her new home staff members saw her bestow a vacant, rejecting attitude on disliked family visitors, only to relax and chat coherently, later in the day, with somebody who was in favour with her.

This is an example of the use of senility as a strategy by some old people. The strategy is not always as deliberate as this, nor is silence the only form it takes. The person who is no longer in complete control of his body and his environment may have only one sure response left in his own hands, the 'non-response response'. 'Stubborn', we may complain, or 'senile'. But he is making use of one of his remaining coping strategies: the ability of divorcing himself from pressure and disagreeable reality by refusing to respond as we demand.

Senility as strategy has its dangers. The old person in an alien and disagreeable environment may turn his mind into a sort of kite. He lets out the string, catches a bit of breeze from memories of a happier past, and allows his thoughts to soar away from the drab realities of the immediate situation. Others may recognise in him a quality of disorientation, that he is not where they are. Yet they do not really know where or why he has gone. Potential care-givers may come to care less because they feel out of touch with the old person's personality. He may be given drugs with disabling side-effects. Removed from daily realities, the mind in flight may become increasingly incapable of meeting its own basic survival needs.

The same downhill spiral can occur when social withdrawal is brought about by protective caution. The individual withdraws from stimulation and social interaction out of fear of being hurt physically or emotionally, humiliated or proved incompetent. He assumes a guarded, no-risk position. Again, this position can not only be mistaken for senility, but can contribute to the actual faltering of the mind by its loss of stimulation, experience and mental exercise.

Senility as strategy may be subtly encouraged by others. Psychologists have observed many children who have given an impression of unintelligence because they had been told repeatedly at home or at school that they were dim. When provided with an opportunity to discover their own abilities and to develop them, the children often flourish.

In the same way old people are sometimes treated as if they were unintelligent and not to be taken seriously. Any error they make (or any point at which they differ from general opinion) is taken as evidence. In some institutional environments the old person is better off if he says and does little. Passivity seems to be what the situation requires. Those who move around, speak up or make demands receive brusque treatment and little consideration. Residents learn to be silent, withdrawn, uncomplaining.

Overcoming difficulties

Always time for a good time, despite hard times.

We must realise that the comfort and well-being of an afflicted person can be improved even when a progressive disease process does exist. Environments can be adapted to allow for a measure of independence together with safety. Instead of isolation the person with senile brain disease can be given the opportunity of continued social contact in a warm and friendly setting. I have seen senile women work confidently and competently in a kitchen provided for their use. Research has demonstrated improvements in mental and physical functioning when the senile aged are moved to a socially enriched environment. Damaged brain cells have not been repaired, but the individual becomes motivated to make better use of his remaining function.

Good nutrition and careful use of medication and exercise can also dramatically improve the condition of those with brain disease. There is great satisfaction in seeing serenity, dignity and self-esteem return to an old man or woman who has been treated with respect. We may find ourselves with a person whose strong character or gentle radiance remains intact despite the ravages of illness.

We must also understand the continual effort of a jeopardised and stressed old person to cope with his difficulties and to make the best he can of the situation. Although he may 'confabulate', reporting incidents that never happened, this in itself is a creative though impaired action. It is an attempt to compensate for the gaps carved in a failing memory.

Is she not paying attention to what is happening in this room? Perhaps this is because she is deeply engrossed in events taking place within her own mind and body, problems to be met or resources to be salvaged out of the range of all perception but hers. Even when senile-type behaviour appears quite bizarre and ineffective, it often has the same goals as our own behaviour: to understand, to relieve anxiety, to achieve safety, to feel like a person.

9 A home full of strangers

'I thank the Lord every day for this place. I never knew people could be so kind . . . There is no other place I would rather be. I am perfectly secure here, perfectly content, and very grateful.'

'What's the charge against me, doc? Don't prisoners get told what they're in for? They call this place home? Some home! We have to get up when they say, eat when they say, go to bed when they say. If you have the wrong expression on your face they stuff a pill down your throat. Is this what your home is like, doc?'

These two statements were made by residents of the same institution for the aged. The same place may, in fact, be quite a different experience for different people, depending on their backgrounds, needs and capacity to adjust. There are also so many differences between one 'home' for the aged and another that generalisations can be misleading. With these limitations in mind, let us look at some of the more important psychological aspects of living in a home full of strangers.

Shelter from the storms

Board games bring people together in groups and give them a reason for communicating.

Weathering the storms of old age sometimes needs the kind of shelter that an institutional setting can provide. Generally it is the older old person who is institutionalised. In the USA, for example, the average age of those in nursing homes is about 82.

In many nations today, the population balance is shifting and the number of old people increasing.[1] This means that the old-age 'home' will be with us for years to come, whether we like it or not.

The process of institutionalisation

This jargon word suggests something heavy and massive. And the process of institutionalisation does mean far more than simply moving someone from one physical place to another.

During the settling-in period the old person has to come to terms with all aspects of his new environment. Perhaps the fact

A modern institution for the aged; for some, a secure haven – for others, a prison.

Adjusting to the idea of a move to an institution can arouse deep anxieties and apprehension.

that this process is known as institutionalisation rather than individualisation makes it clear that the person must adjust more to the 'home' than the 'home' will to him. It is a difficult process, at any age.

Before the move

The upheaval often begins long before the old man or woman even arrives at the new home. Something has already gone wrong, otherwise he or she would not be moving. It may be illness. It may be the loss of a protective person or place to live. Something disturbing has happened or threatens to happen. This means that already both the old person and the family are likely to be vulnerable and perturbed. Anxiety and dread are strong words, which can be fairly applied to this time. Although institutionalisation is seen as the solution, it can make the family feel guilty and the old person feel abandoned. This may not be objectively true in any way.

The family may have been doing its utmost with available resources to help the old person. And the old person may be just as distressed at seeing himself a burden as he is at the prospect of the move. Nevertheless, the emotions are there.

After years of living as an integral part of the family, the old person now faces a wrenching separation. Added to this anxiety is the dread of what the institution will be like. Is it a place to live or a place to die? Can one bear to spend those final years among strangers in a strange place?

Many studies of institutionalisation in old age show how important are the psychological changes that take place before institutionalisation. Sheldon Tobin and Morton Lieberman[2] studied 100 people on a waiting list for entry to a home for the aged in a large metropolitan area. There was one comparison group of 35 old people living in the community and not anticipating institutionalisation, and another comparison group of 37 who were already institution residents.

Better in than waiting

They found that many psychological characteristics of the institutionalised aged *were already shown by those on the waiting list.* Among the people on the list, Tobin and Lieberman found '... a tendency toward apathy, condoning or passively accepting what life has brought, somewhat negative feelings about having accomplished what is regarded as important, plus tendencies towards self-criticism, depression, bitterness or irritability.' There are at least two possible overlapping explanations. Deterioration of the old person's life situation can cause the kind of feelings described above, and also adds to the likelihood of institutionalisation. The prospect of the move can also be depressing in itself.

The study also found that the people on the waiting list had more problems and limitations than those who had been living in institutions for more than a year. Those who had settled in for an extended stay were found to be more emotionally responsive, less anxious, and more efficient in mental functioning than old people on the outside still waiting to move in.

Lieberman and Tobin concluded: 'Most of the psychological qualities attributed to the adverse effects of entering and living in an institution were already present in people on the waiting list.' These findings cast doubt on the assumption that institutionalisation always and permanently undermines mood and mental functioning.

Threats to identity

Anxiety and dread sometimes reach new heights as a person actually enters the institution, even if he or she decides to put a good face on it and avoid making a scene. Weeping in private, staring at the wall, loss of appetite and other signs of distress may follow later, despite best intentions to be content with the move.

The impact of the move can be softened in many ways. In some places, staff members of the institution visit the old person's own home several times before admission to get to know them and answer questions. Sometimes, the prospective resident visits the institution.

The individual may take with him his cherished possessions, which help give a sense of continuity and identity. Staff members may make special efforts to reassure the newcomer, and other residents are actively welcoming and friendly. Simple measures such as these do not alter the significance of the move, but enable the person to feel less isolated, less among strangers.

Devotion to a pet can forge a closer relationship than younger people have time for.

Unfortunately, well-meaning staff members sometimes add to a newcomer's distress by an inappropriate show of familiarity. They are not fully aware of the crisis of identity that the old person is experiencing. He has already lost some of the components of his usual lifestyle and one of the few remaining firm clues to his identity is his name. Yet a perfect stranger may bypass the newcomer's proper name and proceed immediately to a first-name greeting. Mrs Donaldson is transformed into Elizabeth, or more likely into Beth or Bessy. She may be even further reduced to an all-purpose, Dearie or Love. This may seem a small matter, but it exemplifies many of the little–big ways in which institutionalisation makes its inroads. There may be only one Mrs Donaldson in the institution, but dozens of 'Honeys' or 'Dearies'. The name is detached from the person and replaced with a generalised term that does not acknowledge the individual's unique self. The message is clear: 'Who you were before does not count for much here. Just slip into the identity we give you and we'll get along fine.'

The pressure of the institution upon the individual is by no means limited to homes for the aged. The sociologist Erving Goffman and others have shown that similar processes take place wherever a person is almost totally controlled by the environment: in prisons, mental hospitals and military establishments, for example.[3]

Although all these differ from a geriatric institution in important ways, they also have much in common. The inmate's

103

previous identity is replaced by a number or rank. Symbols of the former self, such as clothing and personal possessions, are replaced by others from the establishment. The daily schedule meets the needs of the institution more than those of the individual. Privacy and intimate relationships are not favoured: group behaviour, conformity and surveillance are more usual.

The older person entering an institution for the first time – and knowing it may be his last dwelling place on earth – may naturally experience these aspects of institutional life as personal onslaughts against his integrity. The onslaught, of course, is usually quite impersonal: it is just the way the system works. Individual staff members may have the well-being of the residents very much at heart, but nevertheless function along the mechanical channels of a 'total' institution. A 'total' institution is defined as one in which the residents spend all their time in the same setting, with little opportunity to escape into an environment that might restore a sense of individual identity. Although it provides some of the security needed for survival, it also undermines psychological security by taking so much out of the control of the individual.

Some old people prefer to remain part of the mainstream – others are happy to conform to institution life.

Settling in: the need for caution

Social gerontologist Ruth Bennet and her colleagues have found that most newcomers to institutions receive very little help to make a compromise between his or her previous life habits and the structure of the institution.[4] The rules are often not made clear at the start. Sometimes there appear to be no explicit rules at all, although any institution must have rules of some kind. It appears to the newcomer that there is very little the residents are expected to do, and few roles that can bring personal satisfaction and gain social approval. In all too many settings, the less the person does, the better. This is a very difficult situation in which to learn and adapt at any age.

The early days of institutionalisation, then, may be marked by confusion, by excessive caution ('What if I do something wrong and make them angry?'), and by little incidents that unfairly establish a reputation that sticks ('She's a stubborn one!' 'He's confused!').

Some take more readily to living in groups, preferring others to run things for them. It gives them a sense of security and helps them to relax. People like this have often had earlier experience in other institutional settings and know how to 'learn the ropes' and make the best of the situation. But those who have lived much more private lives are ill-prepared by experience or temperament for this type of arrangement.

Games are often a useful vehicle with which to overcome problems of institutionalization.

The early days of institutionalisation are critical. The old person's anxiety about separation from home, and dread of what awaits him, may intensify any existing physical, psychological and social problems. It is a time when the 'home' should provide the most sensitive and comprehensive care. There is a sense of disruption from one's previous life, and the feeling that there is no road back is acute – and accurate. Thus when the possibility of institutionalising an old person arises, it is vital that the most suitable institution is chosen. There must also be ample social and emotional support during the critical period after admission.

A new found family

Those who settle into long stays at homes for the aged often find friends among other residents and staff and eventually regard them as family. This is an interesting phenomenon.

It seems most likely to occur when family visits become infrequent or cease altogether or when stability among the institutional staff allows personal relationships time to develop. Residents are genuinely comforted by the presence of their new family, and staff may also go well beyond mere job requirement in caring for the 'grandmother' or 'uncle' they have come to love. The situations sometimes seem to represent a triumph of humanity over the impersonal institutional process.

A newfound friend can mean a new-found family

Nevertheless, loneliness, social isolation and the heavy tedium of having nothing to do characterise many old people during extended periods of institutionalisation. This is more likely to be true in large homes and seems to happen when the institution gets beyond the size of a large private house. The difference between a 100-resident and a 500-resident home in terms of psychological adaptation may be less than the difference between a 25- and a 50-resident home. This is now well known to many administrators, and more attempts are being made to establish smaller residential settings in which everyone has a greater opportunity to feel at home.

Limiting adaptation

The Lieberman–Tobin research mentioned earlier also raises the question of exactly what normal adaptation is. After all, residents have to adapt into 'too much of a world of sickness and death', as Lieberman and Tobin put it. A resourceful old person in long-term homes may even become depressed when adaptation *succeeds*. It is adaptation to limits. It is identification with the infirm and failing. It is acknowledgement of death to come. 'I'm not a dead man,' one resident told me. 'But I wouldn't call myself a living man either.' The person who appears not to be adjusting to institutional life may at least command some attention because he does not fit in.

We should, therefore, not take too simple a view of adaptation to life in a home for the aged. And, of course, the pattern of relationships there can be as complex as human relationships anywhere else. Happiness or contentment may hinge upon the ups and downs of one or two close friendships or sworn enemies.

A middle-aged man may return from work in a bitter or frustrated mood because someone else was given the office with the view, the promotion, or the holiday at a favoured time. In the same way, his aged parent in an institution may be either angry or jubilant about his new room or choice of room-mate, or any other event that affects his day. Some things do not disappear simply because a person enters an institution. It is easier to understand why an old person is feeling 'up' or 'down' when we comprehend the importance of everyday incidents, linked as they are with physical difficulties and a longing, perhaps, for the world outside.

New outlooks on institutions

With good facilities, he has discovered an ability with his hands he never knew he had.

Institutions for the aged are changing.[5] Staff is better qualified, facilities are more varied. The best also respect the individual lifestyles of the residents, as far as any institution allows. Some even attempt to introduce elements of life outside, such as sheltered workshops, congenial pubs and clubs for people with common interests.

There are also signs that thought is being given to alternatives to institutionalisation. Home-care organisations are helping aged people to remain in the community, looking after people where they live, without requiring them to move to a home. These services can be as simple as assistance in shopping or meals-on-wheels. The possibilities of such means of helping old people to maintain their style of life have not yet been fully explored. It is likely that in the future an increasing number of people will receive the kind of practical assistance that will help them avoid institutionalisation.

However, there comes a point in the lives of some old people when physical disability increases beyond the reach of either individual or social coping. The very old and very frail will probably always need to be admitted to institutions. Long-term homes will probably become increasingly committed to people who need total care. Despite the progress that can be anticipated in psychological, social and medical–nursing care, there will always remain a large group of aged people who **require** the most basic care.

10 Taking our leave

The look on the face of the five-year-old as he boards a school bus for the first time, and the look on the face of his mother . . . The last, lingering touches of lovers who cannot bear to let each other go . . . The moment when one must board the jet and fly off to a new life elsewhere . . . The apprehension that this could be the last time we shall see each other, the chill of final separation.

Death itself may be an unknown, but separation and loss is a harsh reality for both those who must go and those who must stay. We have a lifetime of thoughts, feelings and relationships behind us when we eventually take our leave. Our experiences with separation and all our feelings for each other come to the fore in our last phases of life.

There may be anxiety and despair, or there may be a new-found sense of intimacy and completion.

A good death?

Scientists prefer to avoid terms such as 'good' or 'bad'. A leading psychiatrist, Avery D. Weisman, who is involved in terminal care, has offered the concept of an 'appropriate' death.[1] By this he means the kind of death that the person would have chosen for himself, given the option. He is allowed to depart from life in a manner consistent with his own values and style. An 'appropriated' death, on the other hand, would have meant that his death had been taken away from him by force of circumstance.

Most deaths today occur in some kind of institutional setting. More than four out of every five people who die in old age spend their last days in a hospital, nursing home or other type of institution.[2] Their lives tend to become part of the institution's workings rather than a continued expression of their own distinctive patterns.

Terminal illness often brings about a loss of function and strength which intensifies the dependence on the socio-physical environment. It has been said that 'we die the death of our diseases', referring to the specific physical and psychological changes caused by diseases such as kidney failure, coronary disease, pneumonia, lung cancer, and so on. But we also die the death that follows most naturally the contours of the environment.

*Grief and remembrance
are not morbid, but
therapeutic.*

Two old people approaching death with the same physical problems will have completely different experiences if one is in an impersonal institution and the other in an institution with a shared lifestyle. This second person may be a nun who lives and dies in the same convent school–retirement home complex, or an orthodox Jew, dying amongst companions who faithfully carry out the prescribed practices and rituals.

These contrast sharply with routine care-giving in an environment that offers no special attention to the values of the individual terminally ill person.

Treat a person, not a disease

The old person's death may be 'appropriated' from him outside institutional walls as well. Some doctors treat diseases yet bypass the individual. Information about his condition is shared only with one or two family members. Decisions are made with little or no consultation and actions are carried out with a minimum of preparation and explanation. In taking away the responsibility, credibility and control of the old person himself, we also set up a situation in which much of his life has become the property of others long before the process of dying begins.

The terminally ill old person deserves to live and die as he himself would choose. Simple though it may seem, this concept runs counter to much in our social and health care network. It is easier to treat 'diseases' and to look after 'geriatric patients' than to work intimately with each person's individual needs as a person.

The need to be open

There are many other factors that make it difficult to achieve what we shall continue to call (for want of a better term) an 'appropriate' death in old age. These include the following:

1. Health care of the aged has become a major budget item in many countries. There is reluctance to spend any more than is 'necessary', and the definition of 'necessary' is seldom in the hands of the elderly themselves. Any new programme of improved care for the terminally ill elderly that threatens to cost more is likely to run into determined opposition. Those nations without adequate health-care programmes for the relatively healthy old person are particularly resistant to 'investing' in the dying person.

2. Many of us (including health care-providers) assume that we *know* what old people and dying people want. This assumption is often a projection of our own thoughts and feelings upon the other person. 'When I get to be that age, I'll be ready to die,' a young person may think. 'She'd rather be out of her suffering,' is another variation on that theme.

This assumption may also be constructed out of bits and pieces of observation. 'I don't want to go on like this,' may be interpreted as a desire for death when the person is actually lamenting the poor quality of his current existence. 'I won't be around long,' may be interpreted as a plea for attention or a 'morbid preoccupation', when it is a simple acknowledgement and notification. Whatever the source of our assumption, it provides an excuse to avoid close contact with the terminally ill old person. Since we already 'know' what he wants and what is best for him, we do not have to be with him, to listen to him carefully and to share his thoughts and feelings about the end of life.

'He doesn't know' and 'It's better that way' are both assumptions that interfere with achievement of an appropriate death. The first is based on the premise that the terminally ill old person is too confused or senile to be aware of his situation. Yet research has shown that awareness of impending death is common, even if it is sometimes expressed in ways that escape our notice. Communication between a dying person and others is subject to extraordinary omissions and distortions. Even direct statements may be 'not heard', 'forgotten', or re-interpreted by the listener.

The idea that the dying old person should be 'protected' from knowledge of his condition often serves to protect others from the uncomfortable prospect of a conversation about dying and death. Since many terminally ill people know or suspect the truth, this evasion does not accomplish a protective function. Instead, it leads to increased isolation and gives the dying person the feeling that it is best to keep his knowledge or suspicions to himself. An opportunity to discuss the situation, clear up misunderstandings and express preferences is lost.

3. Our deaths as well as our lives affect other people. An 'appropriate' death for a person may depend upon the actions of other people, and the nature of the death may influence their lives for a long time to come.

It is not unusual, for example, for one close family member to believe that life-sustaining efforts should be restricted at a certain point, while another believes that everything possible should be done to keep the person alive. Both people may believe they are advocating precisely the kind of action the dying himself would prefer when the old person's wishes are not consulted or not taken seriously. The likelihood of the dying person achieving an 'appropriate' death is greater when there has been a pattern of continued, open communication among patient, family and professional care-givers.

General theories, no matter how firmly based, cannot take the place of direct contact with particular people. We put the books aside when we approach this unique person whose life is drawing to an end. Guidelines drawn from clinical experiences and research are only useful if they supplement the good sense and emotional honesty that a helping person can bring to the situation.

Pomp and ceremony, solemnity, anger and joy: funerals in Bali, London, Athens and New Orleans show the different attitudes of different cultures.

Dealing with a unique person

His house is fitted with handrails to steady his footsteps.

Any prolonged illness is apt to influence our mental functioning. Sheer fatigue is one important element. Mental alertness wavers and it is difficult to sustain attention and thought. Efforts to remain at least partially self-sufficient drain the energy and almost everything becomes harder to do. Pain and other physical discomforts also reduce the available mental energy. The energy remaining for mental functioning is devoted to a few basic problems or needs. There is just not enough mental energy to waste on matters of secondary importance.

The mental changes are often seen as indications of senility or 'how dying people think'. In fact, most people show mental changes when their bodies are depleted and not functioning well. The mental consequences of physical distress are by no means limited to the dying old person. If we simply accept that negative mental changes are an inevitable part of the dying process, we are less likely to seek ways of preventing or alleviating these changes. We are also less persistent in our efforts to maintain good communication with the dying person. This lack of support increases the probability that the person will continue to drift away and the downhill process is accelerated.

Reduced stimulation from other people deprives the individual of here-and-now reality for his mind to work on. At a time when his inner bodily signals are distressing and his outer senses are diminishing, he has an increased need for significant interactions and objects to help maintain mental functioning.

In a world of his own

When a dying person senses that he is being abandoned and that others no longer feel he is worth their time and effort, he is likely to show very understandable mental and emotional reactions. He becomes demanding and agitated or more depressed. He thinks and talks in ways that may come across as peculiar to others. For whenever patterns of communication deteriorate, it becomes increasingly difficult for an isolated person to speak logically.

Unfortunately, reactions of this type often provoke responses that compound the misery. Depressed because he feels abandoned, the terminally ill person may stop eating. Sensitive caregivers may recognise the psychosocial dynamics involved and increase their efforts to provide a sense of affection and security. Less sensitive people, however, may immediately resort to forced feeding through intravenous needle or gastro-intestinal tube. Or they may decide the person is ready to die and let him perish of malnutrition.

There is another fairly common reaction to the distress expressed by the terminally ill old person. Depressed, fearful, trying to find some way to counter the loss of a normal human environment, he may behave in a way that makes him, in some

113

people's eyes, an ideal candidate for mind-influencing drugs. Instead of receiving a human response to his distinctly human needs and distress, he may be pacified by drugs. This approach reduces some of the symptomatic expressions of distress (especially those that disturb other people on the scene) but gives little true comfort to the person. Drug treatment can be part of an effective, comprehensive approach to caring for the terminally ill person – but it can also be misused and become a further obstacle to meaningful communication.

Attention to mental changes can make us more aware of important changes in physical condition. Research shows that the mental functioning of old people tends to become more constricted several months prior to death.[3] This obviously does not apply to all cases and there are people who die suddenly without any advance warning in terms of mental functioning. There are others who have temporary episodes of reduced functioning but who regain physical and mental health.

Signs in advance

Nevertheless, mental changes in old people are sometimes the first signs of a terminal decline. Awareness of this can help us provide more appropriate care for the individual, and encourage sensitivity to his needs and wishes.

Psychological studies have revealed that thoughts, feelings and actions may change when an old person is close to death. His physical condition may appear stable. The psychological changes, however, may take place before there are obvious physical indications of impending death. 'Terminal drop' – an aloof-sounding phrase – refers to a characteristic decline in mental functioning when an old person is a few months or a few weeks away from death.

Two people of the same age may function at the same

Georgians survive longer than any other group. Many live to well over 100 in excellent health. Yet even they must face the end.

intellectual level. Six months later, one shows a decline in performance on a variety of mental tests while the other holds steady. Research findings suggest that the person whose mental functioning has declined is more likely to die soon.[4]

A quality of agitation may appear in speech and manner. Behaviour may be inappropriate to the situation. Mental contact with the environment may become disarranged. Premonitions of death are often expressed indirectly. My colleagues and I in a geriatric hospital, for example, learned to pay special attention to patients who had been in fairly stable condition when they started to give away prized personal possessions, or to place telephone calls to long-unseen relatives.

Professionals as well as lay people have made the mistake of regarding a patient showing this behaviour as senile. Terminally ill old people have been misdiagnosed as mentally ill and shunted into closed custodial wards, where they have spent their final days without sensitive medical or nursing care and away from the people and places who had been part of their lives.

They are left alone with their sense of disintegration. We respond only to the changes in thought and behaviour, using perhaps the good old stand-by's: 'senile', 'confused', 'stubborn', and so forth, missing the opportunity to comfort, and to share one of the most intimate of human experiences.

Some chronically ill old people show a dramatic improvement in mental functioning shortly before death. A person who has seemed confused and out of contact for a long time suddenly becomes lucid and in control of his life soon before his death.

In two realms

The tendency for mental functioning to decline does not mean that the dying old person is without thought and feeling. Our own geriatric research indicates that most people retain a significant degree of mental functioning, and some continue to be alert until the very end of life, unless put under heavy sedation.[5]

The dying old person is usually more alert and responsive with the people with whom he has a special relationship. He is also likely to be more alert on some occasions than on others. Mental functioning is more selective and fluctuating than at other times of life, but often the terminally ill old person can comprehend and experience far more than others expect of him.

It is not unusual for the person to be in two realms, either alternately or at the same time. He can be in contact with the world around him and with his practical needs. At the same time, he may also be engrossed in another reality in which past meanings dominate without the logic and rules of everyday life. The person who spends some of his remaining time in his private world of reality is by no means peculiar or psychotic. His inner world is, in many respects, more meaningful for him than the institution or 'sick room' that comprises his immediate environment. A sensitive companion will respect the dying person's presence in both the world we all share and his own world.

What does a dying person need?

Throughout this book we have tried to achieve a balance between individual characteristics and what is common to most of us as we grow old. This balance also applies to the psychological needs and potentials of a terminally ill old person. Few of us seek pain and abandonment; few of us wish to dwell in depleted or threatening environments. Whatever we understand about human relationships and about helping people when they are in a situation of special vulnerability is applicable to most terminally ill old persons.

Yet each person has his own specific personality resources and needs. We do not relate to an abstract 'old' or 'dying' person but to a very special individual who deserves consideration on his own unique terms.

As death approaches, a person may be flooded with feelings and experiences from the past. Some memories can be painful. The person may recall how somebody else died many years ago, and hope that some of those conditions do not exist for him. There may be memories of disagreements, rivalries, petty misdeeds, and good deeds left undone. Helping the person to share some of these concerns can provide a useful release. He may need the chance to explain why he did or did not do something. There may be a request for forgiveness – or perhaps a family secret that must now be passed on to somebody else. Even if we know the person fairly well we may not recognise what situation from the past is troubling him most at a certain time.

Leaving his life in proper order
The dying person may have simple requests to make which allow him to feel he can leave his life in proper order. Sometimes this involves messages and the distribution of small items to certain

She can't get out to see people – now they come to see her.

116

people. Sometimes it involves certain aspects of the funeral arrangements. He may be concerned about the welfare of the survivors: 'Look in every once in a while on George; he's so absentminded'; 'Fanny's never learned much about handling money; would you give her some help with the bank and the insurance?' Most messages and requests are either practical or sentimental. The dying person does not ask to be made young or immortal. Nor does he expect the listener to perform miracles. He merely wants help to round off a life.

People are sometimes afraid to enter into conversations with the terminally ill, especially if the topics of dying, death and funerals come up. Part of this hesitation is based on concern that such talk will only depress or frighten the dying person. Yet often it is his own apprehension or difficulty in facing death and acknowledging the plight of the dying person that interferes with communication. This deprives the dying person of an opportunity to converse and maintain an active relationship with people important to him.

Many of the dying person's concerns require time. He needs time to think things through. He needs to talk about them several times, in different ways, perhaps to different people. He needs time to make arrangements. Clinical experience and research has shown that people do not move through an automatic sequence of thoughts and feelings before they die, although it is true that some psychological reactions are seen fairly often.[6]

The functioning of a person during a terminal illness largely depends on who he has been throughout his life, the type of condition afflicting him, the type of treatment being received, the special characteristics of his present environment, and many other factors. We can relate better to the terminally ill old person if we do not load ourselves with expectations but approach him simply as the person he is with the person we are.

Grief and bereavement

How does the death of one person affect another? In recent years much has been learned about grief and bereavement. It has been found that even young children can have deep reactions to loss and may show the effects decades later. Attention is most often given to the effects of bereavement when both the deceased and the survivor are relatively young. But the death of old people makes an impact as well. The death of a mother is still the death of a mother even though she may have been 90 and her daughter nearly 70. The power of basic human relationships is not necessarily diminished by the passage of years. Even the death we think we are prepared to accept may leave us feeling empty and shaken when it does happen. If we assume that all old people are 'ready' to die, then we sometimes also assume that their loss will not count for much with the survivors. Accordingly, there is

Grief can be more over-whelming at a public occasion, while private mourning takes longer to assuage.

little in the way of social support during the psychological aftermath of the loss.

The wife-become-widow is the person most often placed in this situation. Wives tend to outlive their husbands, and elderly widows do not often remarry. For many women there is the difficult period of anticipating her husband's death, followed by the impact of his loss, and then the challenge of trying to carry on alone. This is often complicated by financial worries, her own health problems, and social patterns which tend to exclude the un-coupled old woman.

Sometimes the elderly widow is alone with her grief. Self-help groups like the organisation 'Cruse' can give enormous help if the bereaved can find them, but society in general does not yet take seriously the impact of an old person's death.

'*The last time I saw my father, I guess I knew it might be the last time. We talked a little about this and that. Nothing important. It was as if we both had agreed to keep it that way because we both knew and we knew that we knew.*

'*As I started to go, I started rearranging his pillow and blankets, I don't know why. I found myself saying, "Good night! Sleep tight!" just the way he used to say that to me when I was a little girl and he would be tucking me in. I don't know what made me do that and I was afraid I had done something wrong, said the wrong thing.*

'*But Daddy just looked at me with the nicest expression on his face, a private little smile there. And he repeated and finished it: "Good night! Sleep tight! Don't let the bed bugs bite!" That was my Daddy. And that's a moment I won't ever forget.*'

118

Ageing
in perspective

During a recent conversation with a woman who was close to her 100th birthday, I asked her what she made of her life in general. She promptly replied: 'Can't tell yet! I'm still making my life!'

Only a few days previously, a skeptical young psychologist had been with us as a workshop participant. She found it hard to believe that psychotherapy or counselling could be realistic with this age group, but had decided to look into the matter any way. Part of the workshop programme required the participants to introduce themselves to a resident of our institution and spend some time with this person. The young psychologist returned – but the skeptic did not. Again: that glow! 'I never met anyone like this man! He made *me* feel so good. What a person he is. I feel like he's given me some of his own life as a gift . . . Would you mind if I came back to see him again?'

Yet the question: 'What point is there in being old?' is one that constantly hovers about us. Society often behaves as though old people have less intrinsic value than others. Many of us joke uncomfortably about 'getting on in years' or try to conceal signs of our advancing age. The term 'old' itself has become as much stigma as classification.

The prejudice that old age is a worthless, miserable state is virtually guaranteed to poison us throughout our life span. What value can adulthood hold, if it is bound to give way to such a valueless state? We need a more positive view of ageing and old age if we are not to live beneath a shadow of fear and depression for many of our younger years.

Throughout our lives, we want our own respect as well as the respect of other people. We want to be useful. We want to be able to enjoy new pleasures, accept new challenges, be a part of the present and future, as well as the past. We want to function up to our potential, from overpowering physical needs and from excessive anxiety and stress.

It sometimes seems as though old people have more than their share of all these problems. Yet they also sometimes have more than their share of psychological help at their disposal. And almost every helping procedure that effectively copes with human concerns is successfully applicable to the problems of the aged. Psychotherapy can be helpful to old people. Family therapy 'works'. Poetry and art therapy 'work'. Given the skill and sensitivity of the clinician – and the willingness to provide a service to an old person – therapies of many types can be helpful. Residential arrangements have been devised in which old people share co-operative housing with younger people, to the mutual enrichment of all. Foster-grandparent programmes have brought satisfaction to both partners.

For many centuries in many parts of the world it was the oldest people around who were responsible for transmitting history, value, culture. Without this tradition, each generation would have had to stumble about and attempt to create its world anew. Today, despite modern media for communication across time and space, the old person's role as communicator remains important. Books, television, films, computers all store and convey information. Yet only a real person can touch us with the distinctive feeling of a particular generation. A real person can bring the past forward into the present, helping us understand our places as participants in the ancient procession of life. A real person can also model the possibilities of our own old age for us. Here is no packaged media representation of the past (with its direct or indirect commercials), but an authentic human being whose very existence spans past, present, and future. Perhaps this is one of the reasons why so many children and young people in our society seek the company of old people, if they are given a chance to be with them in a reasonable environment. The sophisticated child of today increasingly asks, 'Is it real?' as he encounters a world of slick packaging and subtle deceptions. The child who delights in the company of an old person knows he is in the presence of reality.

Old people are not only valuable to the rest of us. They can also be valuable to themselves. The old person who disregards the negative attitudes of society can often experience a solidly-grounded sense of value. Among our elders today are many who have overcome significant adversities, who have raised families under very difficult circumstances, opened territories, started enterprises, contributed energy and ideas that have helped to shape the present and future. The accomplishments are real; they deserve the respect of the old person him/herself as well as of others. There is also special satisfaction and fulfillment in seeing one's children and grandchildren rise tall in physical and spiritual stature. Children can represent the renewal and continuation of values precious to the old person.

An old person does not have to look exclusively to the past. Opportunities for self-actualization and pleasure often can be found. Many people have been too busy, too weighed with practical life responsibilities to pursue special talents and interests. The businessman may derive more satisfaction with easel and brush than he did in closing sales; the previously house-bound housewife may flourish as a political organiser. The old person may gradually come to appreciate the freedom from hectic schedules, the stress of competitive work, the monotony of daily routines that hold one captive to job or home. Fortified by many years of experience and knowledge, the old person may have a much better idea of how to make the most of time than was the case in his or her youth.

Not all the satisfactions of the old person are restricted to the philosophical or creative. Enjoyable physical activity with its added benefit of health preservation, remains quite possible for most of us in our later years.

Old people sometimes have a greater sense of freedom in the expression of their thoughts and feelings. Anger may be expressed with such forthright candour that it takes others by surprise. The same may be said for affection and joy. Love often shines undisguised from an old man or woman – because it is *there*, and there is someone available to receive it. One of the extraordinary characteristics of some old people is their ability to transmit affection and a sense of joy in life without having to belabour through the 'reasons'. It is as though some of the complex and unnecessary psychological ritual that constricts our expression of feelings throughout much of life falls away: feelings and values can be revealed more clearly.

There was a time in my own life when I wondered about the value of growing and being old. No more. I do not want to miss my old age any more than I would choose to have skipped childhood or adolescence. But I do feel an increased sense of responsibility to this future self and to all those whose lives may cross my path. What kind of old man will I be, given the chance? The answer to that question largely depends on the kind of person I am right now. For growing old is an ongoing project of self-actualisation through the life-span.

Perhaps, in the end, moments to treasure are the same at any age.

References

1 How old is old?

1. Kastenbaum, R., Derbin, V., Sabatini, P., & Artt, S. 'The Ages of Me': Toward Personal and Interpersonal Definitions of Functional Aging. *International Journal of Aging & Human Development*, 1972, 3, 197–212.
2. Butler, R. N. *Why Survive? Being Old in America.* NY: Harper & Row, 1975.
3. Palmore, E. *The Honorable Elders. A Cross-Cultural Analysis of Aging in Japan.* Durham, N.C.: Duke University Press, 1975.
4. Neugarten, B. L., & Hagestad, G. O. Age and the Life Course. In R. H. Binstock & Ethel Shanas (Eds.), *Handbook of Aging and the Social Sciences.* NY: Van Nostrand Reinhold Co., 1976, 35–37.
5. Birren, J. E. The Concept of Functional Age, Theoretical Background. *Human Development*, 1969, 12, 214–215.
6. Nuttall, R. L. The Strategy of Functional Age Research. *International Journal of Aging & Human Development*, 1972, 3, 149–152.

2 Our body and its seasons

1. Birren, J. E., Butler, R. N., Greenhouse, S. W., Sokoloff, L., & Yarrow, M. R. (Eds.). *Human Aging: A Biological and Behavioral Study.* Washington, D.C.: U.S. Government Printing Office, 1963.
2. Timiras, P. S. Aging of Tissues: Alterations in Collagen and Immune System. In P. S. Timiras (Ed.), *Developmental Physiology and Aging.* NY: Macmillan, 1972, 450–461.
3. Kohn, R. R. Heart and Cardiovascular System. In C. E. Finch & L. Hayflick (Eds.), *Handbook of the Biology of Aging.* NY: Van Nostrand Reinhold Co., 1976, 281–317.
4. Barrows, C. H., & Roeder, L. M. Nutrition. In C. E. Finch & L. Hayflick (Eds.), *Handbook of the Biology of Aging.* NY: Van Nostrand Reinhold Co., 1976, 561–581.
5. Timiras, P. S., & Vernadakis, A. Structural, Biochemical and Functional Aging of the Nervous System. In P. S. Timiras (Ed.), *Developmental Physiology and Aging.* NY: Macmillan, 1972, 502–526.

3 The mature mind

1. Hall, G. S. *Senescence, the Last Half of Life.* NY: D. Appleton & Co., 1922. Reprint edition: NY: Arno Press, 1972.
2. Horn, J. L. Organization of Data on Life-Span Development of Human Abilities. In L. R. Goulet & P. B. Baltes (Eds.), *Life-Span Developmental Psychology: Research and Theory.* NY & London: Academic Press, 1970, 424–467.
3. Botwinick, J. *Aging and Behavior.* NY: Springer, 1978 (2nd Edition).
4. Terman, L. M., & Oden, M. H. *The Gifted Group at Mid-Life.* Palo Alto, Calif.: Stanford Univ. Press, 1959.
5. Maduro, R. Artistic Creativity and Aging in India. *International Journal of Aging & Human Development*, 1974, 5, 303–330.

4   Awareness of the passing years

1. Kastenbaum, R. The Old Person: In Stereotype, Reality, and Potentiality. In R. Kastenbaum, *Humans Developing: A Lifespan Perspective*. Boston: Allyn & Bacon Co., 1979.
2. Giambra, L. M. Daydreaming Across the Lifespan: Late Adolescent to Senior Citizen. *International Journal of Aging & Human Development*, 1974, 5, 115–140.
3. Costa, P. T., & McRae, R. R. Age Differences in Personality Structure Revisited: Studies in Validity, Stability, and Change. *International Journal of Aging & Human Development*, 1977, 8, 261–277.
4. Harris, L., and associates. *The Myth and Reality of Aging in America*. Washington, D.C.: National Council on the Aging, 1975.

5   A place apart?

1. Carp, F. M. Housing and Living Environments of Older People. In R. H. Binstock & Ethel Shanas (Eds.), *Handbook of Aging and the Social Sciences*. NY: Van Nostrand Reinhold Co., 1976, 244–271.
2. Cumming, E., & Henry, W. E. *Growing Old*. NY: Basic Books, 1961 (Reprint edition: NY: Arno Press, 1979).
3. Havighurst, R. J., Neugarten, B., & Tobin, S. S. Disengagement and Patterns of Aging. In B. L. Neugarten (Ed.), *Middle Age and Aging*. Chicago: Univ. Chicago Press, 1968, 161–172.
4. Johnson, G., & Kamara, J. L. Growing Up and Growing Old: The Politics of Age Exclusion. *International Journal of Aging & Human Development*, 1977, 8, 99–110.
5. Shanas, E. & Hauser, P. Zero Population Growth and the Family Life of Old People. *Journal of Social Issues*, 1974, 30, 79–92.
6. Richard, S., Livson, F., & Peterson, P. G. *Aging and Personality*. NY: Wiley, 1962.

6   Disaster or challenge?

1. Gunderson, E. K. E. & Rahe, R. H. (Eds.), *Life Stress and Illness*. Springfield, Ill.: Charles C. Thomas, 1974.
2. Kalish, R. A. (Ed.), *The Dependencies of Old People*. Ann Arbor, Mich.: University of Michigan-Wayne State University Institute of Gerontology, 1969.
3. Storandt, M., Siegler, I. & Elias, M. F. *The Clinical Psychology of Aging*. NY: Plenum Press, 1978.
4. Kramer, M., Taube, C. A., & Redick, R. W. Patterns of Use of Psychiatric Facilities by the Aged: Past, Present, and Future. In C. Eisdorfer & M. P. Lawton (Eds.), *The Psychology of Adult Development and Aging*. Washington, D.C.: American Psychological Association, 1973, 428–528.

7   Love and intimacy in later life

1. Pfeiffer, E. Sexual Bahavior in Old Age. In E. W. Busse & E. Pfeiffer (Eds.), *Behavior and Adaptation in Late Life*. Boston: Little, Brown, 1969, 151–162.
2. Lopata, H. Z. *Widowhood in an American City*. Cambridge, Mass: Schenkman, 1973.
3. Butler, R. N., & Lewis, M. I. *Sex After Sixty*. NY: Harper & Row, 1976.
4. Rubin, I. *Sexual Life After Sixty*. NY: Signet Books, 1965.

8   The shadow of senility

1. Brocklehurst, J. C. (Ed.), *Textbook of Geriatric Medicine and Gerontology*. Edinburgh: Churchill/Livingstone, 1973.
2. Butler, R. N., & Lewis, M. I. *Aging and Mental Health* (2nd edition). St. Louis: C. V. Mosby & Co., 1977.
3. Cooper, J. E., Kendell, R. E., Gurland, B. J., Sharpe, L., & Copeland, J. R. M. *Psychiatric Diagnosis in New York and London: A Comparative Study of Mental Hospital Admissions*. London: Oxford University Press, 1972 (Maudsley Monograph No. 20).

4. Lawton, M. P. & Nahemow, L. Ecology and the Aging Process. In C. Eisdorfer & M. P. Lawton (Eds.), *The Psychology of Adult Development and Aging*. Washington, D.C.: American Psychological Association, 1973, 619–674.

9   A home full of strangers

1. Hauser, P. M. Aging and World-Wide Population Change. In R. H. Binstock & E. Shanas (Eds.), *Handbook of Aging and the Social Sciences*. NY: Van Nostrand Reinhold, 1976, 58–86.
2. Tobin, S. S. & Lieberman, M. A. *Last Home for the Aged*. San Francisco: Jossey-Bass, 1976.
3. Goffman, E. *Asylums: Essays on the Social Situation of Mental Patients and Other Inmates*. Garden City, NY: Doubleday, 1961.
4. Bennett, R., & Nahemow, L. Institutional Totality and Criteria of Social Adjustment in Residences for the Aged. *Journal of Social Issues*, 1965, 21, 44–78.
5. Kosberg, J. L., & Tobin, S. S. Variability Among Nursing Homes. *The Gerontologist*, 1972, 12, 214–219.

10   Taking our leave

1. Weisman, A. D. *On Dying and Denying*. NY: Behavioral Publications, 1972.
2. Lerner, M. Why and Where People Die. In O. G. Brim, Jr., H. E. Freeman, S. Levine, & N. A. Scotch (Eds.), *The Dying Patient*. NY: Russell Sage Foundation, 1970, 5–29.
3. Lieberman, M. A. Psychological Correlates of Impending Death: Some Preliminary Observations. *Journal of Gerontology*, 1965, 20, 181–190.
4. Riegel, K. F., & Riegel, R. M. Development, Drop, and Death. *Developmental Psychology*, 1972, 6, 306–319.
5. Weisman, A. D., & Kastenbaum, R. *The Psychological Autopsy: A Study of the Terminal Phase of Life*. NY: Behavioral Publications, 1968.
6. Kastenbaum, R. *Death, Society, & Human Experience*. St. Louis: C.V. Mosby Co., 1977.

Suggested further reading

Hendricks, J., & Hendricks, C. D. *Aging in Mass Society*. Cambridge, Mass.: Winthrop, 1977.
Knopf, O. *Successful Aging*. NY: Viking Press, 1975.
Cowgill, D. O., & Holmes, L. D. (Eds.), *Aging and Modernization*. NY: Appleton-Century Crofts, 1972.
D. S. Woodruff & J. E. Birren (Eds.), *Aging: Scientific Perspectives and Social Issues*. NY: D. van Nostrand, 1975.
Sarason, S. B. *Work, Aging, and Social Change*. NY: The Free Press, 1977.
Carp, F. M. *Retirement*. NY: Behavioral Publications, 1972.
Troll, L. E., Israel, J., & Israel, K. *Looking Ahead: A Woman's Guide to the Problems and Joys of Growing Older*. Englewood Cliffs, N.J.: Prentice-Hall, Spectrum, 1977.

Index

Photo credits

Aliza Auerbach—50 (*bottom*); Ron Chapman—43, 56, 66, 82, 90 (*left*), 102, 106; H. Chokhonelidze—114; Colorific: Linda Bartlett—72, Terence Spencer—112 (*bottom right*); Colorsport—13 (*bottom*); Tony Duffy—4; Branco Gaica—64; Alain le Garsmer—5; Peter Goldfinger—118 (*right*); Henry Grant—9 (*2*), 14 (*right*), 19 (*bottom*), 22 (*bottom*), 34, 41, 46, 48, 50 (*top; middle*), 62, 63 (*bottom*), 78, 100, 107, 113; Ray Hamilton—14 (*left*); Geoff Howard—74; Alan Hutchison Library—8 (*top*); Keystone—14 (*middle*); Judy and Kenny Lester—8 (*bottom*), 70 (*2*), 93, 104 (*top*); Laurie Lewis—13 (*top*); Lisa Mackson—21, 29, 36, 37 (*bottom*), 43, 45, 54, 55 (*top*), 65 (*bottom*), 69, 71, 79, 89 (*2*), 90 (*right*), 96, 99, 101, 105; John Moss—77 (*right*); Moshe Orbach—65 (*top*); Pacemaker Belfast—11 (*right*); Polyvisie—73; Colin Poole—103; Popperphoto—15 (*left*), 47, 59; Rex Features—61, 67, 85 (*2*), 86, 118 (*left*), 121; Suomen Kavapalvelu Press Agency—19 (*top*); Homer Sykes—38, 51, 104 (*bottom*), 112 (*middle*); Syndication International—76, 77 (*left*), 87, 91, 109; Topham—31 (*2*), 33 (*top*), 53, 116; Topix—11 (*left*); Patrick Ward—16, 44 (*2*), 57; WHO—15 (*right*), 26, 55 (*bottom*), 63 (*top*); Val Wilmer—112 (*bottom left*); Zefa—33 (*bottom*), 37 (*top*), 80, 112 (*top*).